PENNY
LANE AND ALL THAT

*For Austen and Imogen who,
thanks to my parents' kindness,
also spent many happy times in Liverpool
during their childhood.*

PENNY LANE AND ALL THAT

Memories of Liverpool

ANN CARLTON

y Lolfa

First impression: 2017

Cover photograph: Painting by Geoff Swinney
Cover design: Y Lolfa

ISBN: 978 1 78461 369 3

Published and printed in Wales
on paper from well-maintained forests by
Y Lolfa Cyf., Talybont, Ceredigion SY24 5HE
website www.ylolfa.com
e-mail ylolfa@ylolfa.com
tel 01970 832 304
fax 832 782

Contents

Preface

I AM FORTUNATE not only in my city of birth, but also in my family and friends who have encouraged me to write this book. I am grateful to them and to my husband, Denzil Davies, who has listened to us reminiscing for many hours.

Geoff Swinney painted the cover picture of Penny Lane roundabout as it was during our childhoods. I am very grateful to him and particularly for the sense of place it conveys.

I am grateful to my cousin Jean Scott (previously McLean) and to my school friends – Irene Brightmer, Anne Morris (previously Griffiths), Judith Stammers (previously Hall) – for their encouragement and for searching attics and backs of cupboards to find photographs from our shared childhoods. Jean provided the photograph of her friends in the sixth form room at Aigburth Vale High School, while Anne went out of her way to take the photographs of the statues at Lime Street Station and the recent picture of the Penny Lane roundabout.

Thanks are also due to Revd John Morris, now of Anglesey, who served as Rector of Holy Trinity Wavertree for many years and who has supplied me with photographs of that church.

I should like to thank Roger Hull of the Liverpool Record Office who helpfully researched a number of the photographs of old Liverpool for me.

I have made every effort to track down the copyright owners of the photographs that I have used, but I am writing about a long time ago and sadly many people have died or cannot remember things well.

To be born and grow up in Liverpool is something special. It can provide you with a sense of humour as well as a dogged determination to fight for fairness and justice. I hope this book gives a sense of that and perhaps of the reasons why the city is so special.

Liverpool –
a very special city

WHAT IS IT that makes Liverpool so special? It is a city that tugs at the heartstrings. It is a city whose name is known throughout the world.

Over half a century ago, like many Scousers born during the Second World War, I left Liverpool to go to university. I never went back there to live. Yet part of me always yearns to return.

The Welsh would call my unrealistic longing for my Liverpool home 'hiraeth'. It is a feeling shared by many among the Scouse diaspora. Sometimes it is combined with a sense of guilt. We left our special city forever. We miss its river, its buildings, its music, its art, its football, its feeling of togetherness and its sense of humour. We feel sad and helpless when the city's social problems are mentioned on television or the Internet.

Each Liverpool exile returning to the city on a visit, possibly for a funeral or a wedding, seems to have a place which means most to them: a place which gives them a sudden feeling of coming home and belonging to the city once again. For me that special place is the view when I walk out of Lime Street Station and face the imposing façade of St George's Hall, with its classical columns and lions standing guard.

In that great hall, as a child, I went to an early Ideal Home Exhibition. There I watched my mother gaze longingly at a vacuum cleaner, and at all the new machinery intended to make housework so much easier than it had been before the Second World War. In that hall too my father, who became Liverpool's Town Clerk, acted as Returning Officer for various elections.

On the hall's forecourt I spent many happy hours laughing at Professor Codman's Punch and Judy show, and its scenes of domestic violence. Once upon a time, when very small, I believed my father when he told me that the huge forecourt lions roared every lunchtime as the one o'clock gun resounded through the city.

For other Liverpool exiles the sense of being a 'wanderer returned home' centres on a football terrace. Football is part of the city's identity. It is what makes Liverpool special for many people, and not just those born or raised in the city. The football teams – Liverpool and Everton – have fans throughout the world.

In my 1950s childhood each football team was identified by allegiance to a particular form of Christianity. Everton's blue-clad supporters were overwhelmingly Roman Catholics. Liverpool's red supporters were overwhelmingly Protestants. This religious distinction has faded away. Even when it was dominant, Scousers usually preferred their special city's other team to win a match rather than, for example, a Manchester team.

My father often said he could feel the whole city reacting when one of our football teams won or lost. He put this shared reaction down to Liverpool's emotional Celtic nature. Perhaps he was right. Liverpool is special in that, though geographically it is in England, it is not an English city. Liverpool was multicultural before that term was invented. Much of that multiculturalism was Irish or Welsh, with a smattering of Scots.

In the mid-nineteenth century the Irish potato famine forced thousands of starving Irish families to cross the Irish Sea seeking food and a new life in Liverpool. In their poverty, fear and starvation they brought with them a tremendous determination to survive, and a consequent willingness to undertake physical work. Their hard work enabled the Mersey docks to thrive.

At about the same time, Welsh people were trekking into

Liverpool from north Wales. They also were looking for work. My maternal grandmother spoke of a family member who, in the late nineteenth century, had walked from Denbigh to the Mersey in search of a job. My mother also talked about her two uncles who were miners. After the First World War ended they travelled to Liverpool from north Wales, stayed in the city for a few days, then boarded a ship intending to start a new life in Australia.

Liverpool's Welsh immigrants brought with them the Welsh language and a love of music. They went on to build numerous chapels in which they promoted both. However, Liverpool is not just a Celtic city. Foreign-born sailors, employed by the many shipping lines once active in the port, settled in the city during the nineteenth and twentieth centuries, adding to the ethnic and cultural mix.

The Liverpool Chinese community grew as Britain's trade with Shanghai and Hong Kong developed. For me, growing up in Liverpool soon after the Second World War, going to a Chinese restaurant for a celebration meal seemed a natural thing to do. Chinese food and the Liverpool Chinese community were part of my life. I was particularly impressed by how good Chinese boys were at playing chess. But it was only when, in the 1980s, an engineer friend went to Shanghai to work that I became fully conscious of the close connection between Liverpool and China. Returning from a business trip to China, he said: 'It felt like being home. Shanghai is so like Liverpool.' It is not surprising therefore that, in 1999, the two cities became twinned, describing themselves as 'International Sister Cities'.

African sailors also travelled to the city during the nineteenth and twentieth centuries, and gradually settled down among the other citizens. A considerable amount of intermarriage occurred between the various groups. In my youth, children of marriages between those with dark and those with light skin were often referred to as 'half-caste'. There seemed little criticism involved in the use of the phrase. It was often seen as a statement of fact, just as the term 'mixed race' is today. Far more frowned upon, it seemed to me in the 1950s, were marriages between Roman Catholics and Protestants.

Equally frowned upon, by both sides, were so-called 'mixed marriages' between Christians and Jews. Liverpool had a considerable practising Jewish population during my childhood. Vestiges of that population still exist, though some of the synagogues have closed. Over the years Jews have contributed substantially to the political life of the city, serving as councillors and aldermen on the City Council. Today both Jews and non-Jews seek admission to the Jewish King David High School because of its high academic reputation. The crooner, the late Frankie Vaughan, who was popular in the 1950s and 1960s, was born into the Liverpool Jewish community.

The African sailors who settled in the city brought with them a rich musical heritage, based on drums and a sense of rhythm. This helped develop something else which makes the city special: the clubs and music that today attract tourists to Liverpool in droves.

The city is special not just for its music, but also for the range of its music. The well-known jazz musician, the late George Melly, grew up in Liverpool and played there often. The Beatles will always be associated with the city in which they were born and went to school. Some of their songs, like 'Strawberry Fields' and 'Penny Lane', refer to areas of south Liverpool in which they grew up. The popular singer and TV presenter the late Cilla Black, like the Beatles a protégé of Brian Epstein, was born and grew up in the city too; her vitality was a living expression of the city's love for life.

Liverpool also has a folk music tradition. It developed from the many sea shanties sung by sailors as they left or returned to the Mersey. Traditional songs like 'The Leaving of Liverpool' and 'Maggie, Maggie May' have been joined in the popular repertoire by more recent ones. They include 'In My Liverpool Home' written by Pete McGovern, 'Liverpool Lullaby' by Stan

Kelly, and the yearning 'I Wish I Was Back In Liverpool' written by Stan Kelly and Leon Rosselson, all in the 1960s.

When the folk duo Jacqui and Bridie appeared on the scene and sang in their folk club at Penny Lane, my parents revelled in the songs they sang about Liverpool life. Given his involvement in the city's slum clearance policies, my father found particularly amusing a reference in the song 'Back Buchanan Street', written by Harry and Gordon Dison, to the absence in tower blocks of flats of a back door to put out the cat. My mother preferred their singing of 'In My Liverpool Home', and would smile at the reference to the idea that, with both an Anglican and a Roman Catholic cathedral, the city had a cathedral to spare.

For fans of classical music the Philharmonic Hall and the Royal Liverpool Philharmonic Orchestra make the city special. The present Philharmonic Hall – there was an earlier one – was opened in 1939 with a concert conducted by Sir Thomas Beecham, known to my father as 'Tommy'. The Phil, as it is fondly called in the city, has a long history of illustrious conductors connected with it. Sir Simon Rattle, one of the best-known conductors of the present age, was born and grew up in the city, and served for a time as the Royal Liverpool Philharmonic Orchestra's Assistant Conductor.

In recent years many popular family saga novels have been set in Liverpool. Books by writers such as Lyn Andrews, Katie Flynn, June Francis, Helen Forrester and Maureen Lee centre on the lives of people in the city. Most span a period between the latter part of the nineteenth century and the time of, or just after, the Second World War. These books are interesting partly because the city and its people are interesting.

Liverpool looks outward across the sea: to Ireland, America, Africa, and the East. Its people travel and its children grow up aware that there is a world beyond their city. The fact that key characters in the Liverpool family sagas can credibly be described as travelling to different places and not just staying in one place, contributes to the attraction of many of the novels.

There is another common factor in many of those Liverpool-based novels: the huge wealth gap between rich and poor. Liverpool's wealth gap is not just human; it extends to its very buildings. The slave trade and other aspects of the shipping industry contributed greatly to the city's wealth during the eighteenth, nineteenth and early twentieth centuries. That wealth is reflected in the city's Georgian domestic architecture, in its waterfront, its Town Hall, and in many other buildings.

But much of the city's wealth was built on poverty and exploitation. There was the exploitation of the slaves, sold by African chiefs to Liverpool traders who then transported them across the ocean for purchase and exploitation by American and West Indian plantation owners. There was the exploitation too of the people who worked in the docks and factories that sprung up beside the River Mersey. My paternal grandfather, a Liverpool docker, felt exploited by the ship owners, who lived in affluence and sat behind polished desks, while he lived in near poverty and could not rely on regular work.

Awareness of exploitation, and a feeling that it was wrong, was not confined to Liverpool's exploited. Some of the exploiters also felt guilty. The city benefited from such rich citizens' unease. During the nineteenth and twentieth centuries, faced with the appalling poverty in Liverpool's slums, better-off people in the city tried to do something to assuage their consciences.

As Liverpool's wealth grew, art and museums flourished. Rich donors handed over pictures and artefacts to the city. Parks, with lakes to row on, were opened up and children's playgrounds with swings, see-saws and children's roundabouts were built. Social pioneers were active, setting up baths and wash houses, orphanages and charities to support families. So great was the need, and awareness of that need, that England's first children's society and the world's first public baths and wash houses were established in Liverpool.

Part of the impetus for these and many other good works stemmed from the city's deep Christian tradition. Irish immigrants brought the Roman Catholic Church with them to the city. The Welsh brought the Protestant religion – Methodists, Presbyterians and Baptists. The city also had a lively Anglican tradition. Christian ministers, of all denominations, delivered sermons on the difficulties of rich men entering the kingdom of heaven, and on the importance of loving thy neighbour as thyself.

Born in 1943, I lost count of the number of times in my childhood I heard my parents, seeing somebody badly off, say: 'There but for the grace of God go I.' They could never really believe the luck that had brought them from the relative poverty of the back streets and back entries of Anfield to south Liverpool, with its green parks and large houses. My mother and father were always conscious of the fact that other family members and people they knew were still badly off, simply because they had not had my parents' opportunities.

My father assuaged his conscience by giving away a great deal of the money he earned to the church, to people in need and to charity. Despite having been very well paid – he had held two top local government jobs on Merseyside, serving as Town Clerk of Liverpool and later as Chief Executive of the then Merseyside County Council – when he died he left his widow with a mortgage to pay off. His bank account included a long list of standing orders to charities, and that was on top of the ten per cent of his income he donated to the church.

I did not mind this generosity to others. Knowing there was so much poverty in the city, I too felt guilty because I was comparatively well off. I knew, as well, that my father was much loved and respected. As his daughter I was very fortunate. I enjoyed privileged access to the city's wealthy heritage and to civic occasions and institutions, while simultaneously mixing with family and friends of different races and financial circumstances.

Perhaps Liverpool is a special city because it combines such a range of financial circumstances and traditions. To overcome differences and live in harmony, its citizens tend to concentrate not on their differences, but on their common humanity. This finds its clearest expression in the Liverpool sense of humour.

Human beings often take themselves too seriously and so emphasise their differences when they communicate with each other. In Liverpool there are so many different traditions it is difficult to do that and get on together.

Liverpudlians joke about each other's foibles, and their own. Their laughter breaks down social barriers. Many stage comedians come from Liverpool. My parents' generation revelled in the jokes of Robb Wilton, Tommy Handley, Ted Ray and Arthur Askey. More recently Alexei Sayle, Jimmy Tarbuck, Les Dennis and John Bishop, among others, have added to the nation's laughter. Sometimes, as in the case of Paul O'Grady who was born over the water in Birkenhead, Liverpool humour's special mix of compassion, happiness and sense of the ridiculous crosses the River Mersey.

Liverpool people's tendency to joke about themselves and each other is perhaps why so many comedians come from the city. Sir Ken Dodd's humour is a typical example of the Scouse approach to life. When he sings about happiness being the greatest gift he possesses, he sums up an attitude that has enabled many Liverpool people to survive.

Another source of the city's strength comes from the local people's awareness of their togetherness. If you belong to Liverpool, you belong to Liverpool with other people. Those who are against the city are against you. Liverpudlians tend to stick together and fight for justice. The *Sun* newspaper found this out in the wake of the 1989 Hillsborough disaster, when it made false allegations against Liverpool football supporters. Liverpool, as a city, showed what its people thought of that newspaper and its then editor Kelvin MacKenzie when, en masse, they refused to buy the paper. It took those affected by the disaster until 2016 to obtain a new inquest verdict on what had happened that day in the crush at the Sheffield stadium, but the campaigners for justice never gave up.

This togetherness developed over centuries. It stemmed

from the survival needs of both men and women. In their poverty Liverpool women knew, if they were to survive, they needed to help each other. Neighbours looked after each other's sick relatives in times of emergency. They cared for each other at times of childbirth or a family death.

Children were cared for not just by their own mothers, but also by a network of family, friends and neighbours who knew that one good turn earned another. Children could become as fond of, and as cared for, by neighbours as by their own blood family.

Working in the docks and dock warehouses, Liverpool men also developed a strong sense of interdependence. They tried to ensure their personal and each other's safety by looking out for each other. Down by the Mersey, working conditions were very tough on the ships, on the docksides and in the warehouses. But the dockworkers' conditions were of little concern to the owners of ships and dockside businesses. They were intent on maximising their company's profits, and not on the welfare of their workforce.

Consequently, Liverpool dockers learnt to look after each other. In modern jargon, when a ship was being unloaded, the dockworkers did their own risk assessments. The men learnt that, just because an order was given, it should not automatically be obeyed. Automatic obedience could lead to injury and even death. Out of this concern for each other's welfare developed Liverpool dockers' reputation for stroppiness.

It is not by chance that Liverpool Football Club has as its anthem the song 'You'll Never Walk Alone'. That song is a reflection of a city's sense of community and Liverpudlians' concern for one another.

Laughter, compassion, a love for other human beings and a vibrant cultural life unite the city of Liverpool. This book is a reflection of that attitude, as I experienced it while growing up in that very special city, during and soon after the Second World War.

To Penny Lane

'WE'RE MOVING TO Penny Lane,' my father said.

Today, thanks to the Beatles' song, there are people all round the world who have heard of the Liverpool district called Penny Lane with its roundabout, bank, and barber's shop. But when my father made his announcement, just after the Second World War, hardly anybody outside the city had heard of the place.

At the time I, like the Beatles who later made the district famous, had only recently started primary school. Living then on the other and poorer side of Liverpool, I had not heard anybody mention Penny Lane before. I did not really understand what my father was saying. I vaguely knew the word 'moving' suggested my world was about to change. But why and how?

I felt so safe and secure living in our council house on the wide Muirhead Avenue with its trees and tram lines, stretching from Tuebrook to Norris Green. Our house, number sixty, like so many council houses erected between the world wars, was well built with three bedrooms, an upstairs bathroom and a small garden front and back. Its fabric was better and its dimensions more generous than many private houses built today. The estate architecture was Georgian inspired, with little urns decorating the tops of some of the houses.

In those days people felt lucky to live on Muirhead Avenue. They were proud of Norris Green and the city's new council houses. They blessed the day that the Liverpool Corporation had given them a new clean home and whisked them away from the grime, overcrowding and poverty of the downtown slums.

For many families, rehousing by the Corporation meant

cooking on a cooker rather than a fire. It meant bathing in a bathroom rather than in a metal bath in front of the fire. It also meant having a private inside lavatory – sometimes even two lavatories – instead of using a shared, smelly brick privy with a wooden seat in an outside yard.

Sadly, over half a century later, hope in that once happy area of Liverpool seems to have given way to despair. The once proud Norris Green council estate has become associated with drugs, shootings, and depressing television programmes on gang warfare. Over the years something went wrong.

The very fact that Muirhead Avenue was such a nice place to live seventy years ago was what prompted my parents to feel we should no longer live there. My father was earning more money than he had earned when the Corporation had allocated him a council house. He had qualified as a solicitor and had a secure job with prospects of promotion in the Town Clerk's Department of Liverpool Corporation.

In the mid-twentieth century the job of Town Clerk of Liverpool was one of the two highest paid public sector jobs in Britain. Reflecting this, senior jobs in the Town Clerk's Department were also well paid. It was, my father felt, morally wrong to continue living in a council house when he could afford to buy a house, particularly when so many other families in the city were living in squalor.

For my parents the move to Penny Lane was a major event. They saw it as going up in the world since south Liverpool, where the Penny Lane area is situated, is a relatively affluent area. My father was born in 1912 and my mother in 1914. They both grew up in Anfield, a poorer part of the city. They met and married at St Christopher's Anglican church in Lorenzo Drive, Norris Green. Involvement with running the Protestant youth group, the Life Boys, at St Christopher's church brought them together.

The Life Boys was then the name for the junior section of the Boys' Brigade organisation. The Boys' Brigade is divided into numbered companies. St Christopher's company is the

49th and is part of a grouping known as the Liverpool and District Battalion. When my parents met each other, the Boys' Brigade and Life Boys were the main youth groups for Protestant boys in the city. The Liverpool Battalion then had about 2,500 members.

My mother played the piano for the St Christopher's Boys' Brigade and Life Boy band. She was, like another young woman involved in St Christopher's Life Boys, my honorary Auntie Dorothy, a woman officer in a very male organisation.

The officers of the 49th Boys' Brigade and Life Boys took those Life Boys whose families could afford it to a summer camp on a farm near Mold in north Wales. My mother greatly enjoyed those camps. When talking about them she always made it very clear that the women officers stayed in a farmhouse, while the boys and men slept in tents in a field. Despite these respectable sleeping arrangements, going camping with men was quite a daring thing for young women to do in the 1930s.

The Life Boys organisation was very keen on physical education. Organised gymnastic displays helped the boys to develop physical strength and self-confidence. There was a gymnastics officer for the Liverpool and District Battalion. His activities involved a number of churches. Seventy years later I talked to that officer who still remembered with pride organising a gymnastic display involving the 49th and 50th Liverpool Boys' Brigade companies. It was performed at Lorenzo Drive before the then President of the Liverpool Boys' Brigade Battalion, who was a newly appointed Chief Constable of Liverpool. The Liverpool police were keen to encourage such boys' organisations in the city; it was felt that, like boxing, which they also encouraged, boys' clubs kept lads out of mischief.

Today there are few Boys' Brigade companies left in the city. As with other uniformed youth organisations, the decline in Boys' Brigade and Life Boys membership has been rapid. Even as late as the early 1970s, the annual Liverpool Boys' Brigade parade and Anglican cathedral service was a huge event. The organisation's hymn – 'Will your anchor hold in the storms of life?' – was sung with gusto inside the Anglican cathedral, and sermons centred around the organisation's motto – Sure and Stedfast – struck a familiar chord with many in the congregation. (The spelling of Stedfast, though unusual, is accurate. It was the spelling used at the time.) Outside the cathedral, after the service, lively brass band music echoed through the streets as hundreds of boys marched behind their company flags in front of the cathedral steps, from where a salute was taken.

The experience of running St Christopher's Life Boys gave my parents a wonderful ability to make young children happy, and the skills to run memorable children's parties. It also gave them a lifelong friendship with two other Life Boys organisers with whom they had also gone camping: Ron and Dorothy Filshie. They were the best man and bridesmaid at my parents' wedding.

As Liverpool's population grew during the nineteenth and early twentieth centuries, overcrowded housing and unreliable incomes encouraged many Liverpool slum dwellers to create honorary families who could provide mutual support at times of need. In the downtown slums people looked after each other and each other's children. It was common in the city for children to call adults 'auntie' or 'uncle', even though they were not blood relations. Thanks to this tradition I, like many Liverpool children, had as many honorary relatives as I did blood relatives. Naturally my parents' Life Boys organising friends became my honorary Uncle Ron and Auntie Dorothy and their four children my honorary relations as well.

St Christopher's Church was built in the 1930s at the same time as the Norris Green council estate was first developed. It stood on the corner of Lorenzo Drive. My father told me that Lorenzo Drive had been so named at the suggestion of a council official known by Liverpool Corporation staff as 'Jones Roads'.

Jones Roads was responsible for making suggestions to councillors for the naming of roads and felt it would be nice to have a road named after him. He knew, however, that councillors would understandably never agree to a suggestion of Jones Drive if he put it forward. He, therefore, suggested Lorenzo Drive, not revealing that Lorenzo had been his nickname when he was in college. His suggestion was accepted.

St Christopher's is known as the 'Children's Church' because much of the money to build it was collected between the world wars by children living in the Liverpool Anglican diocese. It is an austere art deco building, very different from the high church St John the Baptist at Tuebrook that is also near Muirhead Avenue, but towards the town centre. St John the Baptist was designed by the Victorian architect G F Bodley and is full of gold leaf and incense. My parents preferred St Christopher's relative austerity.

My mother made it clear she did not approve of the fact that my great-Uncle Jack attended Anglo-Catholic church services at St John the Baptist. Great-Uncle Jack worked downtown as a storeman in the upmarket grocers called Cooper's. We sometimes visited him there. In my memory he is always sitting on a plump hessian sack, his feet firmly planted on the floor and a gold watch chain across his ample stomach.

When great-Uncle Jack died, my mother returned from the funeral at St John the Baptist sniffing and complaining about the church service. It had all been too close to Roman Catholicism for her. Her problem, she said, was not so much the bells and smells. It was the sight of statues that she regarded as graven images, and the men in lace frocks. Now I wonder if perhaps the cause of her sniffing was allergy to incense. She had never encountered incense before. Alas, it is too late to ask her.

In my childhood the divide between Roman Catholicism and Protestantism in the city was depressingly strong. The English and Welsh Protestants generally thought themselves a cut above the, predominantly Irish, Roman Catholics who tended to be poorer than the Protestants and to have larger families. Sadly the Christian message of love thy neighbour could be drowned by words of hatred. Sometimes the inter-denominational hatred could lead to violence. To me, as a child, this mutual religious antipathy seemed out of place in such an otherwise friendly city.

Not until the mid-1970s, with the advent of those great clerics, the Anglican Bishop David Sheppard and the Roman Catholic Archbishop Derek Worlock, did Liverpool's religious tensions really begin to ease. Over nearly two decades the Bishop and Archbishop encouraged Liverpool's assorted Christian denominations to concentrate on what they had in common, rather than on what divided them.

I knew from an early age that we were not Roman Catholics. If I had been historically aware at the time, the fact that our dog was a fox terrier called Cromwell would have been a clue to our family's denominational allegiance. One day, when we still lived in Muirhead Avenue, two Roman Catholic nuns knocked at the door of number sixty and my parents invited them in. As the sisters sat sipping their tea, the dog entered the room. 'What a nice dog' they said, patting him gently. 'What's his name?' Hearing it was Cromwell the sisters reacted with aplomb: 'Wrong house' they said and soon left.

I knew, even aged four, that the people who lived next door to us in Muirhead Avenue were different from us in some ways, and that the cause of this difference was that they were Roman Catholics. However, I did not care about our religious differences. I loved those neighbours completely. Either from instinct or exhaustion, they were always ready to dry a tear and give a hug. In this they were very different from my mother and father who, like many parents at the time, had read a book advocating strict parenting.

The fashionable strict parenting of the 1940s involved feeding babies every four hours by the clock. If the infant cried between feeds it was to be completely ignored. Even the relatively thick walls of our council house could not drown the sound of my hungry crying. My parents found this difficult but continued to abide by the book.

Their solution to the problem caused by my cries was not to pick me up; that would have been contrary to the advice contained in the book and so could have ruined me forever. Instead, they shut me in the front room, closed all intervening doors, installed themselves in the back room, then switched on their newly acquired wireless at maximum volume in the hope it would mask my wails.

No wonder I so enjoyed going next door to visit Nanna and Ganger Butcher who, following the Liverpool custom of honorary families, had become honorary grandparents. Next door the cuddles were not timetabled or rationed. They were instinctive and frequent. Nanna Butcher maintained that when you sent a letter to somebody you loved, you should not just put cross kisses at the bottom next to your name; you should also send hugs. When I was only four she taught me to draw hugs by putting a bending italic sign horizontally above my kisses.

My real grandparents were all Protestants, but they were not all members of the Church of England. When my parents first introduced my grandmothers to each other, it transpired that the ladies had already met. They had attended the same Liverpool Welsh Nonconformist chapel as children. One had been a Williams and one a Parry. Both had been able to speak Welsh as children. Both still kept in contact with relations in north Wales, whose ancestors had not travelled to Liverpool in search of work.

My maternal grandfather was a bit of a mystery. He was brought up as an Anglican because he was a Blue Coat boy, living and learning in the building that now houses the Blue Coat Arts Centre. However, nobody in the family seemed to know, or be interested in, where he had started life. All I was ever told was that his surname was Burton, and the Church of England Blue Coat charity, which was established in 1708 and financed by profits from the slave trade, had rescued him from a life of poverty.

To be a Blue Coat boy when my grandparents were children meant you were either an orphan or came from a family who were so poor they really could not cope. To be poor enough to become a Blue Coat boy in nineteenth-century Liverpool was to be very poor indeed. Disease and malnutrition were rife in the city then and child mortality was high.

In the chasm at the back of Liverpool's Anglican Cathedral, called St James's cemetery, there is a memorial to Blue Coat boys who died around the time my maternal grandfather was a child. The sight of that memorial brings tears to my eyes. They were all too young to die. Given the lack of medical knowledge and widespread poverty at the time, many probably died in great pain and after much suffering.

For the poor Liverpool children who, like my maternal grandfather, survived childhood, it was a blessing to have been brought up as a Blue Coat boy. Thanks to his Blue Coat education my grandfather made good, becoming a bonded warehouseman on the Dock Road. I still have his corkscrew. To save him from injury when not in use, the corkscrew is shaped like a smooth, shiny bullet and has to be unscrewed and assembled before a bottle can be opened. Sadly, however, all I can recall of my maternal grandfather is his tall form standing in the shadow of a doorway in Townsend Avenue while I sat outside the gate in my pram.

My paternal grandfather was a very different sort of person. Though he was short in stature, he was far more memorable, and not just because he lived longer. My mother had no patience with him. 'He was not a stevedore. He was just a docker,' she pointed out one day.

I wondered at the time how she could say 'just a docker'. Grandad's description of being a docker in 1920s Liverpool tore at my heartstrings. It was not only the dangers of loads dropping or metal hawsers snapping and cutting people in half. There were also diseased rats lurking in the ships' holds, gnawing through imported sacks, and waiting to bite a hard-working docker on the hand or in the face.

All that made dock work dangerous. But worst of all, said my grandad, was the casual system of employment that then operated in the Mersey docks. It was degrading and humiliating. It treated human beings almost as slaves. Twice a day, in the morning and early afternoon, dockers had to stand around waiting to be chosen for work or, usually in my grandfather's case, not chosen. Small and scrawny and a smoker, Grandad was the very opposite of the image of a brawny docker. He looked as if he would find it difficult, if not impossible, to lift a sack of potatoes.

Day after day he was rejected by potential employers. Following a morning rejection, and hoping to get work in the afternoon, my grandad and other dockers spent hours sitting in St John's Gardens below St George's Hall. They whiled away the time between the morning and afternoon stands waiting for work, talking and watching people pass by, or reading.

Grandad told me he did not walk home between stands because that way he saved on shoe leather. One day a journalist from a Liverpool newspaper interviewed him as he sat on a bench in the gardens. He told the journalist at length about the hardships suffered by Liverpool dockers. The memory of that interview was one of the highlights of his life, but I wonder if it was ever published.

The degrading system of standing around waiting to be chosen for work twice a day was still operating in Liverpool docks in the early 1960s. By then I was a sociology student at the London School of Economics, and spent vacations studying downtown in Liverpool's magnificent William Brown Library.

In cold weather dockers, waiting between morning and afternoon stands, came into the library to keep warm. The anthropology books in the sociology section were particularly popular with them. Reading about sexual mores in foreign parts was a whole lot more fun than sitting in the cold in St John's Gardens. This was before the government of Harold

Wilson, a Merseyside MP who knew the hardships dockers suffered, passed legislation decasualising dock work.

There was real discontent behind my mother's 'just' in the description of my docker grandfather. During the war, while my father was fire watching on the roofs of downtown Liverpool, she spent night after night cowering with her father-in-law in the glory hole under the house stairs. By then Grandad was going deaf. Like many elderly people, he chose to ignore his own physical deterioration and blamed others for not speaking loudly enough.

Huddled next to her in the dark, while German planes with their deadly bombs droned overhead, my grandfather would mutter endlessly: 'Can you hear them, lassie? Can you hear them?' She could and she was terrified. She was also worrying about the safety of her husband on watch downtown in a city ravaged by German bombs. The constant questioning did not contribute to my mother's peace of mind.

The last German bombs fell on Liverpool on 10 January 1942. I was born on 30 May 1943. As my mother was an enthusiastic advocate of family planning, I believe those dates are not a coincidence; but I would never have dared mention that to her.

What really irked my mother about my paternal grandfather was his inability to make money. Once he had been a clerk earning a reasonable income, but in the economic downturn of the interwar years he lost his job.

He then made the mistake of investing the little money he had in a greengrocer's shop. Grandad was not cut-out to be a greengrocer, any more than he was cut-out to be a docker. Given advice on how to run the business by the shop's former owner, he chose to ignore it. Feeling sorry for people in poverty, he let too many people run up debts on too many slates. Inevitably he went under, and so was forced to turn himself into a not very credible docker.

After his wife died, times became so bad in my paternal grandfather's family that his second child, my father, had to leave the Liverpool Collegiate Boys' Grammar School. He had been doing well in his studies, but he felt he had to give them up, seek a job and start earning. His hopes of following his older sister to university were dashed. If he had stayed at school, there would not have been enough money to house, feed and clothe the family.

After leaving the Collegiate my father received a card from the school addressed to his home in Knocklaid Road, Clubmoor. Quoting the maxims of Bishop Middleton, who served as Anglican bishop of Calcutta from 1814 to 1822, the card set out the principles the school felt should govern their school leavers' future behaviour. Throughout his life he treasured the card with its message 'to help others'. When I hear today's politicians vainly searching for a statement of 'British values', I sometimes wonder what they would think of Bishop Middleton's maxims, written two centuries ago.

Despite the fact that he was bringing in very little money, and spent more time waiting around hoping for work than working, my grandfather still considered himself to be the head of the household. Since, by definition, heads of household were always tired when they returned home, he believed he should not do anything in the way of housework. Years after my grandfather died, my mother still resented the fact that, before she was even engaged to my father, she spent hours on her knees scrubbing the kitchen floor at her boyfriend's house. What really annoyed her was that, while she scrubbed, her future father-in-law looked on and told her how to do the job better.

After leaving school my father was lucky. In the face of stiff competition, he got a job as a very junior clerk in the Town Clerk's Department of Liverpool Corporation. Thus he began to earn money to keep his father, his older sister, who was studying mathematics at Liverpool University, and his younger sister, who was already showing signs of the schizophrenia that would eventually become such a sad burden.

Despite the poverty of his background, fortune continued

to smile on my father, but much of his later success was thanks to his own hard work. He learnt Pitman's Shorthand at night school and thus was able to become a clerk to City Council committees. Mr Bains, a very old-fashioned solicitor and the then Town Clerk of Liverpool, took my father under his wing and encouraged him to take an external law degree from London University. Mr Bains also took my father on as an articled clerk and so enabled him to qualify as a solicitor in 1947.

Gradually, thanks to Mr Bains's early encouragement, my father climbed the Liverpool Corporation career ladder, becoming Liverpool's Assistant Town Clerk, then in 1956 Deputy Town Clerk, and in 1967 Town Clerk. In 1974, after local government reorganisation and the creation of the short-lived metropolitan counties, he became Chief Executive of Merseyside County Council.

To me, the really amazing thing about this transformation from rags to riches occurred after my father retired from what he always described as 'the public service'. In retirement he became a member of the Mersey Docks and Harbour Board, responsible for the very docks in which his father had so often failed to get work. He also served as President of the Blue Coat Society of Arts, an organisation housed in the building within which my poverty-stricken maternal grandfather grew up.

His links with the arts always gave my father particular pleasure and in retirement he was able to indulge himself in art, music and theatre. The works of Liverpool poets like Roger McGough and Adrian Henri are different from the poems of Tennyson, Wordsworth, and Longfellow that my father recited to me in the 1950s on cold winter evenings as we huddled round the fire, but he revelled in them all.

One of my father's favourite sayings was that local government needed to keep a proper balance between sewers and symphonies. He commented on this frequently when, in the immediate aftermath of the Second World War, there was a great deal of emphasis in the city on slum clearance and house building, and the sewers that accompanied such activities.

In his later years, as a contrast to the sewers and house building, my father delighted in encouraging the development of the Everyman Theatre, in the company of Joan Littlewood, Sam Wanamaker and the brothers Sir John and Sir Peter Moores, who did so much to encourage the arts in the city. In retirement too he greatly enjoyed being Chairman of BBC Radio Merseyside, an organisation that over the years has opened up the city's theatrical, musical and poetic talent to a wide audience.

I suspect the honour of which my father was most proud was not his British knighthood, nor his Norwegian knighthood, and not even his honorary degree from Liverpool University. For him the greatest honour was being asked to serve as President of the Liverpool Collegiate Old Boys' Association, the school he had been forced to leave by family poverty and which had taught him so much.

But, when I was five, all that was a long time in the future. Before that we had to move from our council house to the more affluent area of Penny Lane.

At Penny Lane

'Why wasn't the fire station in Penny Lane?' the Beatles fan asked me. She was interested in the reference in that Beatles' song to a fireman. She was also under the mistaken impression that the bank and barber's shop referred to in the song were actually in a road called Penny Lane. I explained that sixty years ago, when the Beatles were schoolboys, there was not much in Penny Lane itself. Nobody I knew then and who lived in the area said 'in Penny Lane'; they used the phrase 'at Penny Lane' to describe where we lived.

For locals the heart of the Penny Lane district was the roundabout, which is not even in the road called Penny Lane. The low building on the roundabout used to be a public transport waiting room and lavatories. In 2016 an extra layer was built on top of the original shelter and the building has been transformed into a restaurant. When my parents and I moved from Muirhead Avenue to Penny Lane, the roundabout was where the clinking and clanging trams turned round at the end of their journeys and then, after their crews had used the roundabout's facilities, set off back in the direction of Old Swan.

Travelling on the trams, locally known as 'Green Goddesses', was a fascinating experience. The seats were wooden and children were expected to stand. The trams and many of the passengers smelt of tobacco. Smoking was not then thought harmful; indeed children were encouraged to collect the cards, featuring things like sportsmen and flowers, that came inside their parents' cigarette packets.

However spitting, often a by-product of a smoker's cough, was considered harmful. On the trams the NO SPITTING signs and messages urging people to trap their germs in their handkerchiefs because 'coughs and sneezes spread diseases', showed that some sources of illness had been officially recognised.

I still have the silver-coloured overhead tram wheel presented to my father in commemoration of the journey of Liverpool's last tramcar on 14 September 1957. The wheel has a civic crest engraved on it, surrounded by the words 'Corporation Passenger Transport'. Four indents on the outside of the presentation wheel show that the Liverpool Corporation intended it to be used as an ashtray.

Heathfield Road, where my parents bought a house, is just one of the roads which open on to the Penny Lane roundabout. Others include the shopping streets Smithdown Road and Allerton Road; the long Church Road that leads past the Blue Coat School and past Holy Trinity Church and the Liverpool Blind School to the Picton clock and Wavertree village; and the residential road called Elm Hall Drive with two churches at its entrance: one Anglican, the other Methodist.

Mr Bioletti's barber's shop was in Smithdown Place, a road that skirts the side of the roundabout. Collecting for Dr Barnardo's one weekend, my friend Mary and I discovered that under Mr Bioletti's barber's pole was a good place to stand, shake our tins and collect money. Mr Bioletti did not mind our presence, and he had a steady flow of customers for us to accost. Little did we know that, years later, a group of local boys called the Beatles would make the barber's shop and the place we called Penny Lane world famous.

For my friends and me, Penny Lane was more than a district; it was almost a state of mind and central to our young lives. To understand that fact, it is necessary to appreciate how very different from today was life for children born towards the end of the Second World War. We did not have many toys. Computers were not part of our lives, but we had much more freedom than children do today.

There were no mobile phones to enable our parents to keep track of us. In the 1950s most young children did not have watches. Watches were expensive and usually not bought until children went to secondary school, if then. Often parents would say to an offspring: 'I'll buy you a watch if you pass the 11+ examination.'

There were no battery-operated timepieces in those days. When children were given watches they had to remember to wind them every day or they stopped. Most clocks had to be wound daily too. This meant that busy or forgetful people were often vague about the exact time. Whenever my mother felt the need for an accurate time she telephoned Tim, the speaking clock. Tim's recorded voice would announce a variation of 'on the third stroke it will be 10.29 precisely'. Armed with this information my mother rushed round the house setting the correct time on all the clocks and on her watch.

Without mobile phones or watches to prompt their return home, when 1950s children went out to play they could be gone for hours. If we wanted to know the time, we really did ask a policeman. There were quite a few around, plodding the streets and talking to people rather than driving about in cars, or whizzing past on motorbikes, as they do now.

In those days parents did not live in constant fear of paedophiles. This was partly because there was not so much geographical mobility. Consequently, people tended to have known their neighbours for years and to know if anybody living nearby was not to be trusted.

Another reason for the low level of parental anxiety was that severely mentally ill people were often confined to mental hospitals and rarely, if ever, allowed out. Care in the community was only just being invented, and medications to treat illnesses like schizophrenia were not as developed as they are today.

The only time I was attacked was at a relative's house by a relative. My screams brought adults running to my help immediately. The assailant's mother consoled me with the gift of a doll's china tea set. My grandmother had taken me to the relative's house, and I later overheard my mother rebuking her on the grounds that: 'You should have known that young

Arnold is not all there.' The incident was then forgotten. Like the war, it was not a pleasant topic of conversation and so not to be mentioned in front of children.

If adults ever felt it necessary to mention paedophilia or sexual assault in polite circles, they were often referred to as 'interfering with'. Equally euphemistically, being confined to a mental hospital was referred to as 'being put away', while pregnancy was frequently described as 'being in the family way'.

The week we moved to Penny Lane a girl knocked on our front door to ask if she could take me to school. My mother accepted her offer with alacrity. I was in the first year of the infants' school and Jean Morris, into whose care my mother entrusted me, was only slightly older than me. Apart from the day in 1954 when we paid a preliminary visit to the grammar school I was to attend, my mother never took me to school again.

My mother knew I was unlikely to be run over, as there was so little traffic on the roads. Nobody we knew had a car and there were no parked cars at the roadsides. The bus and tram routes were known by the older children and limited to main roads. Britain had spent the war years trying to live as far as possible on its own resources and imports were still low. Consequently, there were very few lorries or vans on the roads. Indeed so devoid of traffic were the side streets off Heathfield Road that, when we were not playing in the backyard of 30 Heathfield Road, my friends and I used the pavements and roadways as our playgrounds.

We chalked hopscotch numbers on paving stones and threw bits of slate to show where we should hop to next. One of our favourite street games was Land, Sand, Sea and Ocean. The tools of this game were a low wall at the side of my house, the three pavement slabs next to it and the road gutter beyond. The paving stone nearest the wall was Land, while the street gutter was Ocean. The other two paving stones were Sand and Sea.

Under the rules of Land, Sand, Sea and Ocean, the person who was IT stood in the middle of the road, while the rest of the children stood on the wall. The child who was IT then shouted Land, Sand, Sea or Ocean. The other children then had to jump off the wall and reach the shouted target in a single jump. It was hard to reach the gutter Ocean without falling over, and that was what made the game so exciting. If a child did not reach the shouted target, they had to take over as IT.

Attaching a skipping rope to a lamp-post, then swinging on it out into the street, was another game, which took us into what would now be regarded as a danger area. Safety apart, parked cars would prevent most modern children from playing marbles in the gutter or swinging off a lamp-post, but we did.

We also played Fives in the gutter. That game involved bouncing a small ball while picking up dice, one at a time, between our fingers. In their campaign against nationalisation Tate & Lyle, the Liverpool-based sugar refiners, had flooded the city with dice depicting Mr Cube on one face. We liked Mr Cube. He had a friendly smile and the dice were ideal for small hands to pick up between our fingers as we bounced our ball. We had no idea of the politics behind Mr Cube. I am not sure we even knew the dice were supposed to represent a sugar cube.

On very hot days the tarmac surfaces of the roads sometimes bubbled up with the heat. We spent delightful hours bursting the bubbles with sticks and sometimes, to our mothers' annoyance, with the toes of our shoes.

All the children loved the smell of tar. My grandmother, a chronic asthmatic, said it was good for her chest. When a local road was being repaired, my friends and I would stand on the pavement sniffing deeply as we watched the huge steamroller trundling slowly along and flattening the tar. We also enjoyed talking to the cocky watchmen who, when roadworks were being undertaken in the area, would set up their corrugated huts and coal-burning braziers at the roadside. The watchmen slept in the huts, protecting tools that were being stored inside for use by the paviours next day.

The back entries at the rear of the houses were even safer places to play than the streets, and in those days did not have gates on them. Some people in Liverpool call back entries 'back jiggers'; but we did not do that because we knew we would be told off if we did so, as the phrase was considered a bit common. To be common or do anything common was frowned on by all the adults we knew. The word is still used in the city as a term of reproof and condemnation of what is thought to be vulgarity.

In the back entries we juggled three balls against walls. That was fun, despite the fact that we got told off if our balls went over walls into crotchety residents' backyards. But the back entries tended to contain things we girls thought nasty, like boys playing football and dog dirt, so mostly we preferred playing in the street.

Grand National day proved particularly exciting each year. Double-decker buses to take people from south Liverpool to Aintree lined up in Heathfield Road in a long green line. My friend Mary's cousin was a bus conductor and let us play on his waiting bus. We spent happy times putting our hands on the pole at the passenger exit, then swinging round the pole to the other side of the platform. The aim was to stretch our legs out as horizontally as possible over the gutter and pavement, while not falling off.

Later on Grand National days I always joined my parents in our lounge. Sitting on the green uncut moquette three-piece suite of which they were so proud, we listened to the commentary on the race as it came through the speaker of the walnut wood radiogram. My father was also very proud of the radiogram. He could remember making a crystal radio set before the war and was in awe of the way technology had moved on.

My parents only had a few 78 rpm records to play on their

radiogram, but felt they did not need many. They were content to listen again and again to the deep bass of Paul Robeson singing 'Ol' Man River' and to the contralto Kathleen Ferrier singing the aria 'What Is Life To Me Without Thee?' from Gluck's opera *Orpheus and Eurydice*.

My mother took against Mirabel Topham, the owner of Aintree Racecourse. She got annoyed when Mrs Topham began to phone my father at home to press her case for Liverpool Corporation to support the racecourse. It was not a personal dislike on my mother's part; she simply resented the intrusion into her home life.

In those days talking on the telephone was still something special. Whenever our phone rang, my mother rushed excitedly towards the mahogany table in the hall to answer it, hoping for a chat with a friend. Her disappointment on finding it was Mrs Topham who was disturbing her domesticity was always considerable. I can still see her, standing next to the table and holding the Bakelite phone receiver at arm's length, disappointment blatant on her face, and shouting loudly: 'Stan! It's Mirabel!'

While I was growing up horse-drawn carts were still around. A rag-and-bone man with his horse and cart sometimes tried to collect discarded metal and other unwanted stuff from householders. However, people were still making do and mending in the wake of the war, so he did not have much success.

The coalman was more up to date; he had a lorry. He delivered heavy hessian sacks of coal to our coal shed via the backyard door. After emptying each load, he laid the empty sack down in the yard so my mother could count them all, and assure herself she had not been short-changed.

The haunting sound of a kilted bagpipe player, perhaps a soldier disabled in war, would sometimes echo round the houses as he sought to beg for money. Sometimes gypsies called at our house; they offered what they described as 'lucky white heather' and pegs for sale. My mother had a soft spot for the gypsies. She bought wooden pegs for the clothesline from them and sometimes let them tell her fortune.

Another street visitor was the knife man. He set up his grinding wheel on street corners then shouted out or knocked on doors, asking people if they wanted their knives sharpened. My mother always asked him to sharpen her bone-handled carving knife, the blade of which became increasingly narrow over the years.

The ice man called regularly on my mother's friend, Mrs Hill, who lived round the corner in Cassville Road. He took ice blocks off his small lorry and carried them along the back entries into her backyard; there they were put in an outhouse. How the ice blocks were kept cold and what they were for, I never knew.

Just as for years nobody I knew had a car, so nobody I knew had a fridge. It was only when I went to the London School of Economics in the 1960s that I met somebody who owned a freezer. Keeping food fresh was a battle, particularly in summer. Our house in Heathfield Road was large, its kitchen was off a morning room; a pantry, to store food, led off the kitchen. The pantry was cooler than the kitchen but things did not keep long even in there.

The absence of an ability to keep food fresh for any length of time is part of the explanation for Penny Lane being so important in my school friends' and my young lives. A lot of food was perishable and so had to be bought almost every day. This meant that, in the school holidays and on Saturdays, we often went to the Penny Lane shops with our mothers. When we grew older, we were sent almost daily to buy things from the shops for them during the school holidays. This activity was known as 'running an errand'.

I was particularly fascinated by Woodson's, the grocer's shop. The shop had sawdust scattered over the black and white tiles on the floor. Miss Sedgwick, who lived next door to us, worked there. When we paid her she sent the money and bill in a brass container along a wire to a cashier sitting in a glass-fronted cubbyhole above the shop. In her lofty vantage place, the cashier checked the bill, counted out change and then sent the brass container back along the wire to Miss Sedgwick. Most of the things we bought from Woodson's were wrapped in greaseproof paper. We carried them home in a small bag made of string.

Oddly, though Miss Sedgwick lived next door to us for thirteen years and left her silver to my mother in her will, I never went inside her house. In moving to Penny Lane we had moved into a different social sphere from the council estate by Norris Green. None of the new neighbours became honorary aunties. Even my mother's best friend, who lived next-door-but-one round the corner in Cassville Road, was always 'Mrs Hill' to me. People living at Penny Lane mostly felt financially and socially secure. They did not need to invent an honorary family to survive.

For me the tentacles of what was called Penny Lane stretched as far along the surrounding roads as I shopped with my mother or went on errands. Sometimes I felt that Penny Lane stretched half a mile along Smithdown Road, nearly as far as the entrance to the large field called the Wavertree Mystery. At other times, when my mother went to her hairdresser's salon, or when my father bought her clothes at the up-market dress shop called Winston's in Allerton Road, I felt Penny Lane stretched a similar distance in the opposite direction, almost, but not quite, as far as the fire station near Green Lane. For me Penny Lane was simply where I lived and where I went out with my friends to do things and see things. It was, in many ways, more interesting than school.

Recently I took my husband on a Google virtual tour of the present Penny Lane area. I showed him the Savings Bank, the roundabout, Heathfield Road and the streets leading off it. He was unable to share my nostalgia and commented: 'It's very suburban.'

'That was what the Beatles pointed out in their song,' I

replied impatiently. Penny Lane was indeed suburbia, and at the time I loved living there.

Opposite the Penny Lane roundabout, and near the bottom of Heathfield Road, stood the Liverpool Trustee Savings Bank. It seemed very important to me as a child. In the aftermath of the war, schools and parents encouraged children to save. Primary schools regularly sold savings stamps to children. We stuck the stamps in special books and saved up for events like Christmas.

Though I bought saving stamps at school, I preferred to put my pocket money in the Savings Bank. I particularly treasured its dark red leather-covered metal box, embossed with a picture of Liverpool castle. When the box was full, a cashier at Penny Lane would open it with a key and add the money to my account. The box was very secure and well designed to keep safe the farthings, ha'pennies and threepenny bits I fed into it. From time to time I tried to raid the box with a knife through the teeth of the slot, but I never succeeded in extracting even a farthing.

My friend Mary Delgarno's father went to the other Penny Lane bank on Smithdown Place because that bank had a night safe. Mary and I would sometimes go with him to drop a leather bag of money into the night safe. There were no credit or debit cards then and many people did not have bank accounts. Consequently, most payments were made with cash. Shopkeepers and people who, like Mary's father, collected rent or insurance money found the bank's night safe useful. It meant they did not need to keep large amounts of cash in their houses and run the risk of being burgled.

The local newsagent's shop was near that bank. I was not the only child in Liverpool who saved up their pocket money each year to buy a copy of the *Curly Wee and Gussie Goose* annual. This could be ordered from the newsagent, Miss Bevins. She was the auntie of a boy of my age who was later a fellow student at the London School of Economics: the political journalist Tony Bevins, who sadly died in his late fifties.

Tony's father, Reg Bevins, caused a sensation when, after being elected as a Labour councillor, he crossed the floor of Liverpool Council chamber and joined the Conservatives. He went on to become a Conservative MP for Toxteth and served as Postmaster General between 1959 and 1964.

When we were both studying at the London School of Economics, Tony and I felt we had a common bond, but it was one we did not particularly like. We were unusual among our fellow undergraduates. Our fathers both earned so much money that, though our university fees were paid, we did not get any maintenance grant to study. There were no student loans then, so we had to rely on our parents to keep us. Tony told me he met his father's driver each week on Westminster Bridge to pick up his money. I relied on parental cheques that I paid into my bank account. Both of us felt the arrangements sapped our independence.

The *Curly Wee and Gussie Goose* annuals contained small cartoon-like drawings of the besuited pig Count Curly Wee and his friend Gussie Goose. The drawings told a story through a short rhyming verse that accompanied each one. During the year, between annuals, I kept up with the Count's adventures by reading the *Liverpool Echo*. I sometimes wish the Count would make a comeback, but he would seem very dated in an age of superheroes and *Star Wars*.

Children growing up in Liverpool at the time were fortunate in having a large number of swimming baths to visit. Some of my friends and I favoured the small Victorian Woolton baths, but others liked the larger baths in Picton Road, Wavertree. When I swam a mile at a young age, the manager of the Woolton baths was so impressed he presented me with a threepenny bit he had dipped in mercury. Nobody then knew mercury could be harmful to people's health. From time to time I bit the threepenny bit to see what mercury tasted like.

My swimming enthusiasm had two downsides. One was that my mother and Mr Bland, the head of Liverpool Corporation's baths and wash houses and a neighbour, decided I should train to swim the English Channel. I then endured seemingly endless private sessions in Liverpool's Cornwallis Street baths, training my legs to do six-beat crawl while reciting 'Mary had a Little Lamb'. Fortunately, I eventually developed asthma and the adults were forced to abandon the Channel swim project. I had never really believed in it.

The other downside to swimming was verrucas. All Liverpool swimming children seemed to get them. My friends and I were sent by our parents to the chiropodist at Penny Lane to get rid of them. He would hack away at our feet manfully. It hurt and we always felt we were wasting our time, because we knew the verrucas would return.

Near the chiropodist's was a furniture shop called Leslie Mann. Among the other shops were two greengrocers, two bakers, a butcher, a fishmonger called Huxleys, a bike shop and Pugh's the chemists. Along Allerton Road, a chandler called Appleton's smelt blissfully of firelighters and firewood. Boots the chemists, also on Allerton Road, had a lending library on its first floor. Sometimes, usually on the bookshelves of an obscure charity shop, a Boots library shield-shaped logo can still be found attached to a dilapidated hardback book and I am filled with nostalgia for the dark brown bookcases and the world Boots library opened up to me.

I do not feel so nostalgic about the hat shop run by Mr Davies in the Smithdown Road part of Penny Lane. My mother was heavily into hats for civic occasions and church, especially large hats with large brims. The hats suited her and they impressed others, but I found them deeply embarrassing. Other people's mothers did not wear big hats.

I can still recall my teenage embarrassment when, lying in a bed at the far end of a very long hospital bronchial ward, I saw my mother heading towards me with a huge navy blue cartwheel hat on her head. She was off to an event at the Town Hall and had got special permission to drop in and visit me en route.

On either side of the ward, bed-ridden sufferers from

asthma, bronchitis and emphysema, coughed and spluttered up the contents of their lungs. Full of maternal concern, my mother did not notice those patients; her only interest was in reaching me. Nearer and nearer down the ward she and the hat came. Eyes full of pain followed them. I tried in vain to hide under the bedclothes.

I also hated the hats my parents bought for me at Mr Davies's shop and made me wear for church services and concerts in the Philharmonic Hall. Other children did not wear posh hats. When I pointed this fact out to my mother, she replied that other children did not have a father working in the Town Clerk's Department. There were standards to maintain. We were keeping up appearances.

Near the hat shop was McManus's shoe shop. The shop had an X-ray machine. It was great fun, but nobody realised at the time that it was not good for our health. When you tried on a pair of shoes and the shopkeeper thought they fitted, you were told to step up to the machine and tuck your feet inside. Next, you, your mother and the assistant peered down through a screen at the bones of your X-rayed feet, complete with outline of the shoe and the nails holding it together.

Opposite McManus's was a large Co-op department store. I much preferred buying shoes in the Co-op. The assistants there encouraged my mother to buy me less sensible styles than Mr and Mrs McManus sold. Once, under the influence of a particularly persuasive Co-op sales assistant, she bought me a pair of bottle green bar shoes. I was delighted. I felt they were so much nicer than the sensible brown shoes and sandals I was usually made to wear.

After rationing was abolished and goods became more plentiful, all sorts of things could be bought at the Co-op and, to my mother's delight, there was a dividend too. Our divvy number was 12 93 12. From time to time, I would go down town with my mother to collect her divvy from the Co-op offices near Higson's brewery. The smell of the brewery when it was in action put me off beer for life.

The only shop I went to in Penny Lane itself was the Chinese laundry. We did not use its services for sheets, clothes or tablecloths because our house had its own wash house off the backyard, across from the outside lavatory and next to the coal shed. We had a dolly tub, a mangle, a washboard, wooden tongs to take washing out of the tub and a wooden three-pronged stick to stir the washing. Each washday a washing line to dry the clothes on was strung across the backyard. Once the wet clothes and sheets had been pegged on to the line, it was raised high in the air by a wooden clothes prop.

My mother left washing and ironing to my grandmother, who came to live with us soon after the move to Penny Lane. She seemed to enjoy using little blue bags to get our sheets looking as white as possible. She also seemed to revel in slamming down the electric iron on to the scorched, folded blankets and sheets which were used to turn our morning room table into an ironing board. But even my grandmother drew a line at starching my father's detachable collars and white shirts. They went to the Chinese laundry.

The detachable collars were taken back and forth to the laundry in a leather horseshoe-shaped box. When attached to the starched white shirts by collar studs, and sometimes stiffened even further at the front by bone collar-stiffeners, they became part of my father's office uniform. They were worn with a range of almost indistinguishable dark, pin-striped suits, handmade by a tailor at a shop in West Derby village. In winter my father topped this attire with a dark, heavy overcoat. In his hand he carried an immaculately rolled black umbrella. On his Brylcreemed head he wore a black bowler hat.

As a child I thought he looked very smart heading down Heathfield Road to catch a bus into town. However, in the 1960s, bowler hats began to go out of fashion and some local boys made his life difficult.

The boys thought the bowler hat made my father look like Mr Swindley, the manager of Gamma Garments in the TV soap *Coronation Street*, a part played by Arthur Lowe, who also acted as the bank manager in the *Dad's Army* TV series. As my father walked along our road, the mischievous boys would scamper down the entries parallel with Heathfield Road calling out: 'Mr Swindley, Mr Swindley.' My father saw the funny side of many things; but he failed to share the boys' sense of humour on that. However, I could see the likeness and still have that bowler hat.

In our early teens my friends and I thought it very sophisticated to go to the Milk Bar opposite the laundry in Penny Lane and order an ice cream with cherryade frothing on its top. Sophistication also took the form of buying sticks of cinnamon from the chemist at the Green Lane end of Allerton Road, then trying to smoke them, while hiding from our parents and other adults, in the back entries.

The Milk Bar and Chinese laundry were at the roundabout end of Penny Lane itself. Further along the actual Penny Lane, a bridge passes over the main-line railway between Liverpool Lime Street and London Euston. In those days the London trains stopped at Mossley Hill and not, as now, at Runcorn. Children were expected to think it exciting to stand on the bridge and watch the steam trains pass beneath. When we first moved to Penny Lane my parents sometimes took me to see the trains, but after a few visits I did not find the experience that exciting and instead tried to imagine what it was like downtown in Liverpool's city centre.

Down town

MY PARENTS WERE excited: 'We're going down town window shopping,' my mother announced. I did not understand their excitement because I did not remember the city during the war when all the streetlights were switched off and shop and house windows blacked out. My parents were off downtown because the streetlights had been switched back on and because, while there was still some rationing, shop windows had begun to display goods instead of being blacked out.

It was evening when my parents went out and the shops were all shut, but that did not matter to them. They were not going downtown to buy anything. They were just going to look and revel in the electric light and lack of war. Liverpool had been heavily bombed and large parts of the city centre were wasteland. Undeterred by that destruction, my parents were off out to celebrate the fact that life seemed to be returning to normal in the city centre, at least among those shops that had somehow survived the bombing.

Adults, who we almost invariably described as 'grown-ups', tried to protect children from unpleasant things; consequently they did not talk about the war in front of us. Nevertheless, we were vaguely aware it had happened and that people in Liverpool had suffered a lot. Sixty years after my parents' window-shopping expeditions, my husband picked me a bunch of wild flowers. He thought them beautiful and was stunned when, with an instinctive shudder, I asked him to put them in the compost bin.

'How could you not consider rosebay willowherb beautiful?' he asked.

'Easily,' I replied. Deep down, in my subconscious, there lurked memories of Liverpool's tragic downtown bombed sites, on which pink rosebay willowherb and later purple buddleia thrived. Growing up in an agricultural village in west Wales, my husband had not acquired such an aversion.

One of the downtown places bombed during the war was the Georgian Clayton Square, which was eventually all demolished in 1986. In the remains of the original square, a gigantic Christmas tree, a gift from Norway like the one in London's Trafalgar Square, was placed each year when I was a child.

I have a vivid memory of going with my parents to see a particularly interesting civic switching-on of the Christmas tree lights. All was expectation. A band played. Carols were sung. The Lord Mayor made a speech declaring the lights switched on. He pressed a switch. For a moment the tree lights gleamed and an awed collective sigh rose from the assembled watchers. Then, in a trice, the lights went out. All the lights went out, not just the tree lights but the street lights as well. Suddenly it was pitch-black, just like during the war. People were silent and stunned as they wondered how they were going to get home.

One year when the technology was under control and the Lord Mayor's official switch-on ceremony had gone well, I asked my father if I could press the switch to light up the Norwegian tree. It was arranged for the very next day. I was relieved to discover I could press the switch without making a speech, something I had suddenly begun to worry about. For a small child being able to light up such a huge tree was a very special treat.

There were two ways of getting down town from Penny Lane. One, which my mother preferred, went past the big houses in Ullet Road and Princes Avenue. The other went down the poorer Smithdown Road and along Upper Parliament Street with its large Georgian terraced houses, once the homes of the rich but by then transformed into slums. The two routes met at the Rialto cinema that was eventually burnt down during the Toxteth riots of 1981. My mother used the Upper Parliament Street route to educate me about the things I should, and should not, do.

One of the things I definitely should not do was sit on the front doorstep and chat like people did in the slums of Upper Parliament Street. A front step should be scrubbed regularly with a pumice stone. It should only be used to walk on when going in and out of the house; sitting on it was common, and the last thing a young lady should be was common.

I thought sitting on the front step chatting with my friends would be fun. I did not understand that the people in Upper Parliament Street sat out on their steps because the rooms they lived in were terribly overcrowded. I did, however, wonder why so many women sitting on the steps had curlers in their hair.

There were pubs on almost every corner of the Smithdown Road and Upper Parliament Street bus route into town. They provided my mother with another educational opportunity. She would reminisce about the days, in the 1920s, when her father took her down town on the tram. Through the tram windows her father had pointed out the ragged and shoeless children hanging round pub doors, and explained to her that the children's poverty was caused by the evil drink.

Coming from a bonded warehouseman, her father's denunciation of the evils caused by alcohol must have had quite an impact on my mother. When we travelled together on the bus along Smithdown Road, she too would point out children hanging round pub doors. She said the only difference between that scene during her childhood and mine was that, in the 1950s, the children hanging round the pub doors wore shoes. In her childhood the slum children were often barefoot.

I sometimes overheard people referring disparagingly to the children hanging round the downtown slum streets and pubs as 'guttersnipes'. I found this odd. My friends and I did not see anything wrong with gutters; we often played in them.

Gradually shops filled with goods, wartime restrictions were lifted and my mother took great delight in being able to buy her clothes downtown. She favoured George Henry Lee's, now John Lewis, and another upmarket department store since closed called Henderson's. The shop from which she most enjoyed buying her evening and cocktail dresses, so necessary for Town Hall receptions, was Cripps in Bold Street.

From time to time my mother took me to the top of Bold Street. From there the stark outline of St Luke's church could be seen. It had been bombed by the Germans during the war, and is kept as a, to me rather disconcerting, memorial of the war. In those days Bold Street was reverently referred to as 'the Bond Street of Liverpool' in the same way as Georgian Rodney Street, where private medical and dental consultants were concentrated, was referred to as 'the Harley Street of Liverpool'.

My mother visited other downtown department stores as they restocked after the war. She sometimes shopped at the big department store called Lewis's for make-up and stockings, and she invariably bought her net curtains in a smaller shop called Blackler's. It was socially important to have clean and, as far as possible, crisp nets covering house windows at all times. Maintaining them took a lot of effort because the sooty city air, that blackened the stone of so many downtown buildings, rapidly made white nets turn to dirty grey.

Despite shopping in them, my mother thought both Blackler's and Lewis's a bit downmarket. At the time a popular Liverpool expression – 'standing there like one out of Lewis's' – was a way of describing people who were not being helpful or lively. It probably originally referred to the dummies used to display goods in the shop's window, but some people thought it referred to the sometimes less-than-helpful shop assistants. To describe somebody as 'standing there like one out of Lewis's' was definitely an insult. It was almost as bad as being told you had done something that was common.

Sir Jacob Epstein's statue above Lewis's entrance caused much amusement in our family. It was unveiled in 1956 and formally called 'Liverpool Resurgent', but perhaps more accurately, and certainly more popularly, described as 'Dickie Lewis'. My cousin Jean's mother, my Auntie Nellie, thought it most embarrassing. The man was not just naked; he was also very obviously male and ready for action. Somehow it did not seem suitable for its site over an entrance to a department store, and opposite the Adelphi, which was then considered to be the poshest hotel in Liverpool.

After the statue was installed, my Auntie Nellie was downtown during a Liverpool University rag week. She stopped to watch the student procession of decorated lorries passing in front of the Adelphi. To her surprise, one lorry load of students decided to pay a special tribute to Sir Jacob's statue. As their lorry inched forward a male student, clad only in a cut-off wooden beer barrel, slowly lowered the barrel threatening to reveal parts of his anatomy usually hidden from view. The students may have thought it a laugh and a fitting tribute to Dickie Lewis, but it upset my Auntie Nellie.

My father's shopping trips downtown were rare. He sometimes bought clothes from the men's outfitters Watson Prickard's, and in December he always went with my mother to a shop called Bunney's, which had a magical toy department. There they would buy toy presents to hang on our ten-foot-high Christmas tree: fans from China, little shells which when put in water opened to reveal small waving flowers, paper musical instruments to blow. He also enjoyed visiting the Wizard's Den, a shop that sold jokes and conjuring tricks with which he amused us at family children's parties.

Sometimes my father bought my mother jewellery from Wilkins the jewellers or from the large department store, George Henry Lee, to match her new dresses. I have inherited those family jewels. They look impressive; but, while they might be described in television antiques programmes as costume jewellery, a more suitable word for some of them might be bling.

I thought my mother looked very glamorous as, clad in a long evening dress and gleaming jewels and on her way to the Town Hall, she swept down the bending staircase of our house. Her dark hair was newly permed. Her face was covered in Max Factor Pan-Stik, Bourjois rouge highlighted her cheeks and cherry red lipstick glowed on her mouth. Round her neck she wore a gleaming pseudo-diamond necklace. On her right wrist, over the long evening gloves that stretched to her elbow, a matching bracelet sparkled.

As my father rose to higher and higher office in Liverpool's Town Clerk's Department, my mother went out more and more. She loved the Town Hall with its shining silver tableware and its gleaming chandeliers, and was very keen on how people should behave when they were guests of the Lord Mayor.

In 1964 the Beatles were given the Freedom of the City of Liverpool and a civic reception at the Town Hall was held in their honour. The group appeared, to huge cheers, on the Town Hall balcony. My mother's comments on her return home were not about the Fab Four, but about the terrible behaviour of some councillors' wives. They had lowered the tone by screaming and standing on chairs to get a better view. Their behaviour, she said, had been common. They had let the city down. She was disgusted.

I rarely went to the Town Hall because it was not an administrative office, but a place for City Council meetings and Lord Mayoral receptions. However, one year I was invited to the Lord Mayor's annual children's party. I was about eight. I did not know many other children there, so I spent the visit keeping close to the Alker twins, who were the children of the then Town Clerk, Thomas Alker.

I wore a blue taffeta dress, of which I was initially very proud. It was the first dress my parents had bought for me from a downtown shop. Getting ready for the party, I looked in a mirror and thought my dress very beautiful and special. Later that day, I realised my dress was almost the same as the Alker twins' dresses. It was just a different colour. I was deeply disappointed. I had thought my new dress unique.

For me, the highlight of that Lord Mayor's party occurred when the children, sitting on seats in the Council Chamber, were led by my father in a rousing chorus of the sea shanty 'Sons of the Sea'. Every other line was replaced by the phrase

'Bobbing up and down like this'. We children bobbed up and down on the leather seats with unbridled enthusiasm.

Liverpool's Lord Mayor's coach was in almost weekly use. It was large, well sprung and pulled by horses. The spectacle of the Lord Mayor and Lady Mayoress, with coach and horses, arriving for services at various churches or chapels on Sunday mornings or at synagogues on Saturdays was much enjoyed by Liverpool children. They stood around in the street waiting for the coach to arrive.

The Lord Mayor always wore a red gown for such events and was often accompanied by the Town Clerk in his black velvet, cotton and silk robe with tassels in odd places. The Lord Mayor's gold chain was large and very heavy.

The part I liked watching on such civic occasions was the moment when the Lord Mayor got into his carriage. The springs were good, but the whole carriage could tip sideways if a particularly fat Lord Mayor forgot to move quickly into the middle. I used to wonder if he might fall out.

My father's workplace was the Municipal Buildings in Dale Street. The Town Clerk's Department was located in raised ground-floor rooms on the corner of Dale Street and Sir Thomas Street. As he progressed up the Town Clerk's Department career ladder, my father's office got nearer to Dale Street and eventually he occupied the Town Clerk's Office by the corner. On many a lunchtime he would walk along Dale Street to eat with friends at the nearby Kardomah Café.

I loved going to see my father in his offices. The numerous bound volumes of *Halsbury's Statutes* in the tall glass-fronted bookcases fascinated me, as did the high ceilings and heavy wooden furniture. The adjacent general office of the Town Clerk's Department was a small, busy but happy place. I enjoyed meeting the committee clerks, some of whom had become my honorary uncles.

There were far fewer office staff working for Liverpool City Council then, and they were not as highly paid as local authority administrators are now. I find it difficult to understand how it is that local government seems to achieve less today than it did then, and is less respected than it was then.

The year 1951 was a particularly busy one for the Liverpool Town Clerk's Department. It was the year of the Festival of Britain and Liverpool's celebrations were planned in style. One event was held on the river: numerous vessels of different shapes and sizes tied up at the landing stage or stood in the river. They were dressed all over with flags and hooted in celebration. Aboard a boat, I watched events with my parents as we travelled out towards the Mersey Bar, then back to the Pier Head. The Liverpool fireboat, pumping celebratory river water high in the air, was particularly impressive. Later fireworks soared into the sky, their coloured lights reflected in the murky Mersey water.

One day, during the Festival of Britain celebrations, my parents took me downtown to see Rossini's opera *La Cenerentola*, which is the Cinderella story. I was enthralled. Afterwards I went with them to the Walker Art Gallery where a civic reception was held for the singers and civic dignitaries. It was the most glamorous evening of my childhood: a visit to the opera followed by a party with grown-ups in beautiful clothes and surrounded by the amazing pictures that are housed in the gallery.

Once I entered my teens, my parents allowed me to travel down town on my own. There was so much to see and do downtown. Pocket money could be spent on records at Brian Epstein's music shop, NEMS (North End Music Stores). Sitting in the gods at the Playhouse theatre only cost a shilling and the acting was superb.

I had got past the stage of believing my father's tale that the two large statues outside the Walker Art Gallery were Mr Rushworth and Mr Draper, owners of the Liverpool music store of that name. I knew that, as I walked up the gallery's steps, I was passing statues of Raphael and Michelangelo, though I was not clear why they had been chosen to sit there.

In my teens, I considered myself too old for what had been

a great childhood pleasure: watching Mr Codman's Punch and Judy on St George's Hall plateau. The performances were very exciting and very politically incorrect. Mr Punch was forever bashing his wife Judy on the head. The baby suffered considerable child abuse, and the dog seemed to be fed on strings of fattening sausages. For some reason I never understood, Mr Punch's family had close encounters with a shabby, green crocodile.

As a child I was still able to enjoy the old St John's Market. I have, on my wall at my home in west Wales, an old print of this wonderful building. It had a high roof, tall wrought-iron pillars and stalls whose goods spilt out on to the ground in front of them: fruit, clothes, fish, tools, meat, vegetables. It seemed you could see and buy anything in that old market.

By the market entrance fat, elderly-looking ladies sat on stools. They dressed in long black dresses and wore shawls round their shoulders to keep them warm. The ladies were known as 'shawlies' or 'Mary Ellens'. They held out bunches of herbs for sale and called out: 'Sage-a-mint-a-parsley, lady.' My mother always bought something from the shawlies. She felt guilty that she was so much better off than they were, and in calling her 'lady' they showed they knew it.

Whoever described the demolition of the old St John's Market 'an act of civic vandalism' was right. It was a great asset and the concrete replacement ghastly. Through his then job as Liverpool's Deputy Town Clerk, my father was deeply involved in the planning of the demolition of the old market, and proud of its replacement at the time.

All I can say in his and his fellow perpetrators' defence is that other local authorities were making similar mistakes then, and some are still doing so. Relatively recently, the west Wales county town of Carmarthen pulled down its thriving traditional market and replaced it with a smaller one because the County Council felt the town needed a Debenhams department store. That town's new market is serviceable, but it too lacks the old atmosphere.

In the 1960s elected politicians promoted concrete with

enthusiasm, whether it was for tower blocks of flats, offices, comprehensive schools, motorway bridges or vast shopping centres. My father, as a Liverpool Corporation official, was swept along in that concrete enthusiasm.

The buildings that replaced Liverpool's traditional St John's Market included a tower with a revolving restaurant from where, on a good day, you could see Blackpool Tower and Snowdonia. That was interesting, but I found the food served in the revolving restaurant just as interesting. In Mr Roberts's restaurant at the top of the St John's Tower I first ate a prawn cocktail, as well as scallops wrapped in bacon, while marvelling at the view. Today, when fruit is flown into Britain from countries as far away as New Zealand, Chile and Thailand and supermarkets stock a vast range of goods, it is hard to recall just how boring and repetitious our immediate post-war diet was. However, it was very healthy.

After the war there were still food shortages and money was tight. I grew up knowing each week what would be served for almost every main meal at home. On Saturday we had salad. On Sunday there was roast meat. On Monday it was cold roast meat and chips, and on Tuesday rissoles made from the cold meat. On Wednesday there was shepherd's pie made from the last remains of the Sunday meat. On Thursday it was often tripe and chips, but sometimes it was fried Spam or tinned corned beef and chips. The cooked delicacies were usually accompanied by vegetables boiled to soggy tastelessness in water laced with bicarbonate of soda.

By Friday my mother and grandmother would not know what to give us. However, they always made sure that on Good Friday we had a tin of John West's pink salmon, complete with shiny white bones. I hated that tinned salmon. I much preferred lettuce and white sugar sandwiches, or connie-onnie sandwiches made from tinned condensed milk. A particular delicacy was sandwiches made from soft brown sugar; so tasty and so bad for the teeth. Bread was always white, never brown.

My favourite comfort food was chip butties made with thickly buttered white bread. The chips were cooked in lard and heavily smeared with HP sauce. A battered and blackened chip pan, half-full of used lard, stood permanently on the top of our gas cooker.

My grandmother and mother were devoted to butter. Once rationing ended in 1954, they swamped their toast with it. I knew other children whose parents saved on butter by feeding them salad cream sandwiches, but there was no saving on the butter cholesterol intake while my grandmother and mother were around.

After my grandmother died and food shortages were over, I discovered that my mother was a very good cook. She concentrated on what might be described as homely ingredients, and her braised steak was a particular speciality. However, after my father was appointed Town Clerk, she was not quite sure what to do with the two pheasants he brought home from town one evening.

It transpired it had long been a tradition for whoever was Lord Derby to present whoever was the Town Clerk of Liverpool with a brace of pheasants at the start of each shooting season. My mother had never encountered pheasants before. She took the two birds to her local butcher to have their feathers plucked. Then she roasted them and served the meat in pheasant sandwiches. Family screams of pain soon followed. As we munched our pheasant butties, our teeth closed on the lead shot that had killed the birds. That hurt.

In 1959, my parents agreed I could go down town on my own, two evenings a week, to play chess at Liverpool Chess Club. My late evening walk down to the Pier Head from near Exchange Railway Station, where the club then met, to catch a bus to Penny Lane was solitary, but I was not frightened. I loved to stand alone near the statue of King Edward VII on horseback at the Pier Head, feeling wind and rain blow from the river on to my face and looking up at the imposing buildings of Liverpool's waterfront. In those days nobody had thought of calling them The Three Graces, but they were just as impressive as they are today.

Each year on 12 July the area around Exchange Station was far from quiet. That day Liverpool's Orange Lodges celebrated the Glorious Twelfth of July: the anniversary of the 1690 Battle of the Boyne in which the Protestant Prince William of Orange beat the Roman Catholic King James II.

In the 1950s Liverpool Orange parades were amazing. Horses and ponies, still in use to pull carts around the streets, were borrowed for the day. Young King Billys and Queen Marys sat on them. They were beautifully dressed. At the head of each Lodge, a Lodge banner was held aloft. It usually portrayed the victory of the Battle of the Boyne. Behind the horses and banners, to the beat of numerous drum and fife bands, walked hundreds of Protestant men, women and children.

Liverpool's traditional celebration of the twelfth of July included a trip by train to Southport from Exchange Station, which was closed in 1977. On the sidewalks leading to the station, children waved orange streamers in the air. One year, watching the Protestants march towards the station with their horses, banners and bands, I asked my mother to buy me an orange streamer to wave. She refused and told me I did not understand what it was all about, adding: 'They'll return drunk from Southport too.'

The big Orange marches were sights to see, but I am glad they are now only a memory. The accompanying hatred of Roman Catholic Christians was not something I could relate to. Before I went to university, in 1961, I asked a chess-playing friend, Bill, why he had taken part in those marches which seemed to me to have been so full of hate. His reply, which I paraphrase, was revealing: 'When we lived in inner Liverpool, we had nothing else. Everything else was drab.' I realised then it was glitz and excitement, not hatred, that motivated most of the people who took part in those downtown marches half a century and more ago.

Eyes on my beads

AS HUMAN BEINGS get older they often wonder what happened to the people with whom they were once bosom friends. Musing quietly at home, they ask themselves what happened to the child they held hands with at primary school, the lover they first kissed, the person who worked next to them in their first job. Once, apart perhaps from newspaper and magazine columns trying to put people back in contact with each other, there was little opportunity for many people to find out; but the Internet has changed things.

I had not talked to my primary school friend, Doreen Wood, for over half a century. Then one day, out of the blue, the phone rang and there she was. Doreen's son had tracked me down on the Internet. In a trice we were back at Mosspits Lane Primary School with Miss Lyon, our headmistress, who was kind but very strict.

I found it impressive that Doreen remembered a whole lot more of our early education than I did. She could recall my first day at Mosspits, when I had asked to sit next to her. She could also remember the names of the teachers of our infants' classes. I had to confess that the first teacher whose name I can recall was Miss Forrester. We were in the junior school by the time we entered her class and Doreen and I were eight years old. The only things I clearly remember Miss Forrester teaching us was sewing. We made napkin holders out of beige cloth. I embroidered mine with purple and orange flowers.

Though I wrack my brains, I do not remember learning to read at school. I do, however, remember sitting in front of our lounge fire at home practising reading with my father. Our chosen reading material was reports made to the City Council's Fire Service Committee about major fires. It was thrilling stuff, particularly if there was a fire in the docks. Often then a report would refer to the 'pre-determined first attendance'. The fire engines comprising the pre-determined first attendance would hurry to the fire but find it all too much for them and call for reinforcements.

Later the Liverpool Salvage Corps, an organisation that had done so much to retrieve and recycle goods from the docks and bombed homes during the war, would appear on the scene. The city was very proud of its Salvage Corps and reading about it in the reports added to my excitement.

I do have a very vague memory of endless repetition of times tables while in Miss Forrester's class. I hated it at the time, but that knowledge and the mental arithmetic tests, which were so much part of our young lives, proved very useful in adult life.

What I remember most about Miss Forrester's class is her knickers. In those days women and girls often wore thick knickers that extended to knee level. At the bottom of the right knicker leg, there was sometimes a pocket to store a handkerchief. Miss Forrester wore such knickers. When she needed to use her handkerchief, the class would watch with bated breath as her hand surreptitiously edged up the hem of her dress, seeking the knicker pocket and its content.

One day Doreen and I were in our classroom when a child's loud running steps were heard along the wooden corridor. Abruptly the steps stopped. The classroom door was flung open and a child announced loudly: 'The King is dead.' Nobody said anything. I do not think most of the class understood what the message meant. To my surprise one of our classmates, Catherine, burst into tears.

Mosspits Lane School had a policy that could now be described as 'heightist'. Whenever classes lined up in the playground, they had to line up by height. The tallest was invariably at the front and the smallest at the back. Doreen and I were the smallest in the class and so were always at the back of the line. That meant we were out in the cold and rain longer than our classmates, but the chill wind cemented our friendship.

Miss Lyon, the headmistress, dominated our daily morning Mosspits' assemblies. She insisted we all stood with eyes front. To make sure we did so, she would say: 'Eyes on my beads.' Woe betide the child whose eyes were not on those beads. This was all part of teaching us to pay attention and to concentrate.

Just before I was due to leave that school there was, for me, a particularly awful assembly. The top class was allowed to sit at the back of the hall on Bamco tubular chairs made of canvas and metal. The boys in the row behind me decided it would be fun to tie the ribbons on my plaits to the back bar of my chair. It hurt and I tried to turn round to stop them. In an instant Miss Lyon was on my case: 'Stand up Ann Holmes.' I could not do so. I was attached to the chair. It was the boys who eventually got told off, but I was mortified. I had never liked my plaits. From that day on I hated them.

Over forty years after they were cut off at Pride's Hairdressers, an upmarket hairdressing salon in the original Georgian Clayton Square, I found my plaits wrapped in tissue paper and hidden in a gold painted Lloyd Loom ottoman at my mother's house. She had treasured them. In contrast, I hung my hated plaits from a bush in my Carmarthenshire garden, and for a few years took pleasure in watching small birds pluck out individual hairs to line their nests.

It was not just in the school assembly hall that concentration was demanded of us. Classroom lessons were also designed to develop our concentration. For most of the time we sat in rows facing a blackboard. We were told off if we looked away and stopped listening. We were regularly asked questions about what the teacher had just been saying and were expected to put our hands up to show we knew the answers.

After 'Eyes on my beads' Miss Lyon's second most frequently used phrase was 'Oh! Oh! Oh! There's a sound.' She patrolled the school corridors repeating that phrase loudly if she heard even the slightest whisper. The former MP, Edwina Currie, who was also a pupil at Mosspits Lane, has told of how the headmistress put the fear of God into her at the time. She spoke for all of Miss Lyon's former pupils. We were terrified when we heard our headmistress's approaching Oh! Oh! Oh!s. This meant that well-behaved children frequented the corridors of Mosspits Lane School and there was very little bullying.

A common punishment for inattention was to stand outside the headmistress's room in the wooden building that formed the junior school and learn a poem. I learnt Tennyson's poem 'The Eagle' that way, but did not find learning it much of a punishment. I enjoyed poetry and spent many a happy childhood evening with my parents, sitting in front of a coal fire, reciting Tennyson's 'Lady of Shalott' or Shelley's 'Ozymandias'.

In the junior school at Mosspits Lane, each desk had a white china inkwell filled with dark blue ink at its top right corner. There were no biros, and fibre tips had not been invented. We learnt to write with a metal-nibbed wooden stick pen, which we dipped into the inkwell. This was a messy business and ink tended to get everywhere, particularly on our fingers. The pressure of writing meant we often developed small patches of hard skin on our fingers. We called the patches 'segs' and sometimes, when particularly bored in class, picked at the hard skin.

I found writing clearly in longhand very difficult. My brain seemed to get ahead of my hand. Miss Forrester noticed my failings and did not approve. She did not mince her words. When I was leaving her class, she made it very clear to my parents that I needed to pull my socks up. In my school report, as well as commenting on one subject: 'Good when she works,' she wrote: 'Ann must practise handwriting in the holidays.'

My parents made sure I practised handwriting every day during that holiday, but my style of writing just got worse. Inevitably the 'when she works' was the subject of long parental lectures, on the theme that you only got out of life what you put into it, and I needed to put more into mine.

Miss Forrester's school reports were typical of the era in

their frankness and open criticism. We were at Mosspits Lane School to learn, and praise was only given if it had been hard-earned. When we children took the flimsy, sealed envelopes containing our school reports home, we worried about possible adverse comments written inside them and about what our parents' reaction would be.

As our education at Mosspits Lane proceeded, life got increasingly competitive. We were tested regularly. Not only were we streamed by class, we were also streamed within our classroom. Desks were allocated according to how well we did in regular tests. The cleverest child sat in pole position, on the left hand side of the classroom as the teacher looked at the class.

By the time Doreen and I reached the top class, the positioning of our desks had acquired an external significance. The children nearest the left hand side of the classroom were allowed to take the Margaret Bryce scholarship that was awarded to the eight cleverest children in the whole city of Liverpool, as assessed by examination.

The girls sat the examination at Blackburn House School and the boys at the Liverpool Institute. The winners had to attend these schools to take up their scholarships. In the year I sat the examination, my cousin Catherine won one of the scholarships. She and I were mutually competitive. It seemed obvious to me that if Catherine was going to Blackburn House I could not choose it as my secondary school, so instead I went to Aigburth Vale High School for Girls. My friend Doreen chose to follow her sister, June, to Calder High School, another good girls' grammar school and the sister school of the boys' grammar school Quarry Bank. Our choice of grammar schools was the beginning of our gradually losing touch.

In the 1950s Liverpool was proud of its grammar schools, but the 1960s move to comprehensive schools meant they were abolished. Some of the buildings remained, while others were demolished. Calderstones Comprehensive School now stands where Calder High School and Quarry Bank previously stood.

Blackburn House and its related boys' grammar school, the Liverpool Institute, were both closed down and the Liverpool Institute for Performing Arts was eventually established behind the façade of the former boys' school. Aigburth Vale High School was initially turned into a comprehensive, but was later closed down and its buildings demolished. Today flats stand where the classrooms and playground once stood. The Liverpool Collegiate School, where my father obtained the education that enabled him to escape from relative poverty, was also closed down and the building eventually turned into flats.

Aigburth Vale school's main building was very well designed, with an assembly hall, also used as a gymnasium, at its heart. At ground level, there were classrooms off the hall on two sides, a cloakroom on one side and offices on the fourth side. The offices included the headmistress's study. A balcony, with classrooms off it, ran round three sides of the hall at first-floor level. On each side of this central core were wings containing cloakrooms at ground level and above them rooms for specific purposes – an art room, music room, a library and laboratories.

It was one of the grammar school's great advantages that children stayed in their own form rooms for most lessons. Each girl had a desk within her form room and in it she stored her books. This meant that, between lessons, there was little movement of children round the school. Instead it was the teachers who moved around.

When we did move out of our form room for lessons, like art or science, we did not carry heavy bags. We only took with us the things we needed for the lesson we were going to. The absence of movement between lessons meant that there was little or no bullying. It also meant that we did not strain our backs carrying heavy bags from lesson to lesson.

Like Mosspits Lane School, Aigburth Vale was at first very disciplined, though I noticed, as I grew older that things began to slacken. This was probably the result of a change of headmistress, as well as general changing attitudes in the world of education. Our teachers became less authoritarian. Perhaps I should not complain too much about this, as one of my school reports commented adversely on my 'questioning attitude towards authority'. My cousin Jean, who followed me to the school, still wonders if she would have done so had she known my reputation there. However, the school's organisation did seem to become more chaotic and less conducive to study over the years.

In my mid-teens I upset the new headmistress at Aigburth Vale, Miss Morton. I protested about her announcement at a daily assembly that children wanting to claim free school dinners because their parents were poor, should line up in the hall outside her study. This would have put them in full view of other children coming out of classrooms at ground floor and balcony level. It would have meant, therefore, that everybody would know which children came from poor families.

In those days many people felt a deep sense of shame if they were poor or did not have a job. Shadowy memories of the workhouses still hung around in some families. Receiving benefits was something most recipients hated having to do. After her announcement, I went to see the headmistress. I pointed this out to her and suggested that, instead of queuing outside her room, children needing free school meals should reach her room indirectly, and less openly, via a cloakroom and a secretary's office.

To her credit, the headmistress agreed to that suggestion. It must have been hard for her to back down in the face of a pupil's criticism. However, in the sixth form I was one of only two girls in my year who were not made prefects. I suspected my questioning attitude towards authority had been held against me.

One of the things that also counted against me with those in authority at Aigburth Vale was my attitude to games and gym, an attitude shared less openly by many of my friends. We hated organised physical activity. We could not see the point of climbing ropes or wall bars just to come down again. I was too small to leap over equipment like the dreaded leather horse. Once again knickers featured in my education because, instead of shorts, we had to wear rough navy knickers in the gym. We all felt we were far too old for that sort of exposure.

When we reached the age of sixteen, there was a particularly difficult incident. A photographer from a local paper came to take pictures of our class celebrating the building of a new gym. The teacher told us to drape ourselves, clad in our navy knickers, on the wall bars and other equipment. It then transpired that the young man the local paper sent to take the photographs was not much older than us. Worse still, one girl in our class knew him rather well. We understood her embarrassment.

Unlike gymnastics, tennis was fine as it was an individual sport. The same applied to swimming, but team games were not popular with many girls. I was frankly terrified of the hard hockey balls. If placed in goal, I always ran away when the gang of howling navy-clad girls with sticks approached me. I wanted to live.

At the start of our time at Aigburth Vale my friends and I were particularly proud of our school blazers. We even wore them at weekends and in the school holidays. The blazers showed we had worked hard to get to a good school and, in the days before anoraks, they were very useful.

However, as we girls grew, our school uniform became a problem. Somehow the summer dresses with their gathers at our developing bust levels, bias-binding decoration, Peter Pan collars and puff sleeves lost attraction. In winter the gabardine macs, navy blazers, white shirts and ties we were expected to wear did not seem suitably feminine. Worst of all were the oddly-shaped school berets we had to wear with our winter uniform on journeys to and from school. Any girl caught by a teacher beretless in the street got a telling off and a detention.

For a time I tried to improve the appearance of my school uniform. Beneath it I wore a paper nylon underskirt with coloured net frills. The frills were stiffened with sugar starch to make the navy skirt above stick out. The effect was quite ridiculous, but I revelled in it. Teenage rebellion is an odd state of mind.

The teacher who made the biggest impression on my new friends Judith Hall, Irene Brightmer and me in our first year at Aigburth Vale High School for Girls was a history teacher called Miss Thomson. She thrilled us with tales of ancient Egypt and for a time we all wanted to be archaeologists.

Judith lived in the lodge of Mossley Hill House, which everybody called Carnatic Hall. Both lodge and house have since been demolished and replaced by Liverpool University halls of residence.

The original Carnatic Hall had large wooded grounds. Judith and I loved to wander through them towards the main house. There we could peer through the dusty windows and see a real Egyptian mummy's coffin. The mummy and other valuable artefacts had been stored in the hall by Liverpool City Museum. German bombs had wrecked the museum's galleries in May 1941. Carnatic Hall was just one of the places scattered around the city in which artefacts were stored.

Alas my assessment of Miss Thomson's teaching took a turn for the worse when I was studying 'A' level British history. It was unfortunate that she felt unable to teach the syllabus beyond 1908 and the launching of *Dreadnought*, because the man she loved had been killed in the First World War.

Another 'A' level history teacher, Miss Watson Walker, shared with us her dim view of politicians and their activities locally. William Huskisson, a President of the Board of Trade, had got himself knocked down and killed by Stephenson's railway engine, the *Rocket*, at the opening of the Liverpool to Manchester railway. Not to see a steam engine coming at you could only be described as stupidity, she felt. Viscount Castlereagh had gone and committed suicide; which was not something Foreign Secretaries should do. Winston Churchill, for whom Miss Watson Walker seemed to have a particular dislike, wore siren suits because, she said, he was gaga and could not dress himself properly.

The teaching of 'A' and Scholarship level French and English were memorable in a different way. Both subject teachers encouraged wide reading. In French lessons we read the plays of Molière, Racine and Anouilh. The day our French teacher read out the fifteenth-century poet François Villon's question: 'Mais où sont les neiges d'antan?' and translated it as: 'Oh, where are the snows of yesteryear?' I shuddered with delight. It all seemed so sophisticated. My education in French speaking was, however, far from successful. One day I was rebuked for: 'Speaking French with a Scouse accent.' Thereafter my confidence was utterly destroyed.

We were taught English by Ruth Etchells, who was then a relatively recent graduate of Liverpool University. From Aigburth Vale she travelled up the academic ladder, becoming Principal of St John's College, Durham, and publishing a number of books. She also became a highly influential member of the Church of England, being for nearly ten years a member of the Crown Appointments Commission that nominates Anglican bishops and archbishops.

Studying English with Ruth Etchells was sheer joy. We revelled in the works of T S Eliot, Dylan Thomas and Robert Browning. The lessons were all very emotional. However, the event I remember most from school English studies happened when we were studying Shakespeare's play *Julius Caesar* for an examination.

We were taken to see that play performed by an amateur drama group downtown in the David Lewis Theatre. At the moment of maximum impact, the university academic playing the part of Caesar, stood centre stage. At the top of wide steps, he declaimed: 'Et tu, Brute?'

Unfortunately, he declaimed with such dramatic force that his false teeth shot out of his mouth and clattered down the steps. The academic then proceeded to collapse theatrically forward down the steps, an arm outstretched to reclaim the fallen dentures. Alas, Caesar's next line: 'Then fall, Caesar!' was almost drowned out by unsympathetic teenage laughter.

In my early childhood women teachers usually had to resign from employment when they got married, so most of the women teachers I encountered during my school career were unmarried. The ban on employment of married women was unfair; but it meant that, generally speaking, we had teachers whose main focus in life was teaching us rather than caring for a family. There was no talk then of work/life balance, maternity leave, or family-friendly hours. Our teachers, like the devoted spinsters who staffed many of Liverpool's children's homes, tended to seek fulfilment in their lives through their work.

We did not realise it at the time, but some of our younger teachers' lives must have been affected by the deaths of so many men in the Second World War. In the 1950s many women were not married because the men they might have wed had been killed in the war. Others were war widows, but since grown-ups did not like to mention the war to us, we did not think about that.

Future war was a different matter. We were expected to worry about that. One day, a woman was sent to the school to give us a lecture on what to do in the event of nuclear war. I recall sitting bemused in the art room at Aigburth Vale listening to her list of preparations for such an event. We were told to whitewash our windows and to store tins of food and bottles of water. To me it all seemed highly improbable that we would survive a nuclear blast and consequently a waste of time.

The aim of our education at Aigburth Vale was twofold: to educate us academically and to turn us into young ladies. It seems odd, therefore, that our school song was a poem by Robert Browning that included the line: 'So we battled it like men, not boylike sulked or whined.'

Aigburth Vale School's Biblical text, from St Paul's letter to the Philippians, read out on all great school occasions, was more appropriate than its school song. It was also a valuable lesson on how to make the most of life: 'Whatsoever things are true, whatsoever things are honest, whatsoever things are just, whatsoever things are lovely, whatsoever things are of good report; if there be any virtue and if there be any praise, think on these things.' The school's motto – The Utmost for the Highest – gave us a related message.

Both Mosspits Lane and Aigburth Vale schools were imbued with the Christian ethos. Our daily assemblies included prayers and hymn singing as well as school notices and advice on how to behave. In the lower sixth form at Aigburth Vale we were encouraged to show practical Christianity by volunteering. That was why, one year, I found myself spending Saturday mornings teaching clay modelling at the Victoria Settlement on Netherfield Road, a very poor area of the city.

In the Settlement classroom, the children made very imaginative clay models that some naturally wanted to take home to show their parents. Because the Settlement had very little money, that was not allowed. The models could not be fired because there was no kiln and no money to buy one.

In vain I protested that, by making them destroy their creations at the end of each Saturday morning, we were not really helping the poor children. The children were surrounded by the dereliction of bombed sites and slum clearance. Their physical surroundings were ugly. The children thought the clay models they fashioned were beautiful. I felt that volunteering should involve encouraging a sense of permanence and pride in the children, not demanding more destruction.

My friend Judith and I were much keener on arts than sciences and our teachers noticed this. Soon after Mrs Millet, the physics teacher, discovered I did not want to understand the functioning of an electric bell, I was cast out of physics and chemistry lessons and told to study general science and biology instead. It was made clear that this was a very bad reflection on me, particularly as I was a chess player and quite good at maths.

Judith and I then thought we would like to learn Ancient Greek. Sadly, we did not learn much Ancient Greek because the teacher only managed to give us eight lessons in a year. Upset, I turned to a family friend, Canon Taylor. He had got a first in Classics at Balliol, Oxford, in the nineteenth century. For a year, once a week, the frail old man and I sat in his front room and read St John's Gospel in its original New Testament Greek. Like Latin, the little Greek I learnt has been helpful to me in adult life in understanding and enjoying the meaning of words.

The failure of our school to provide us with the Classical Greek lessons we yearned for was in some ways understandable in the context of the expectations surrounding girls' education at the time. Large wooden boards in the school hall recorded in gold lettering the names of girls who had achieved the highest accolade and got into Oxford or Cambridge. Despite that, it was widely assumed we girls would eventually find our real fulfilment in getting married and having children. Then it was highly likely we would give up work. Consequently, the choice of subjects to study was very much more restricted than it is today.

Guidance on careers given by schools was also rather limited. It seemed to me that the greatest encouragement was given to girls who wanted to become teachers or nurses. Nevertheless, the eventual occupations of girls in my school year included a vet, a doctor, a geographer and a social worker, while former pupils included the late Elisabeth Sladen, the actress who starred in *Dr Who*, and the writer and newspaper columnist Bel Mooney who attended the school until her family moved from Liverpool. I am increasingly curious about what happened to my fellow pupils with whom I lost touch. I hope their lives have been as interesting and happy as mine.

Parks and gardens

EXPERTLY I ROWED through a ragtag of novice punting holidaymakers having a day out in Oxford. I brought the rowing boat alongside a jetty and shipped my oars. Unexpectedly, the boatman left his hut and proceeded to congratulate me. 'I've been watching you,' he said in awe. 'Where did you learn to row?' I was flattered. He obviously thought he was in the presence of a great oarswoman from past times.

The boatman's face fell, however, when I replied: 'Calderstones Park Lake, Liverpool.' He was not to know what good training in the avoidance of boating incompetents rowing on that lake was for girls sixty years ago. Our girls' problem then was boys. They would lie in wait behind an island, out of sight of the park authorities, and try to ram us or rock us out of our boat. They never succeeded, but we all had fun. To be honest, rowing on the lake would not have been the same without the boys.

The boating lake, later sadly devoted solely to fishing, was not the only entertainment Calderstones Park provided. In summer there was an open-air theatre at the back of the white painted mansion house. Sitting in deckchairs, we watched shows that often had an atmosphere of pantomime. Surely it was a man, dressed as a woman, who led us in the memorable chorus:

> How would you like to be middly diddly,
> Bobbing around on the siddly iddly?
> Making chips for tiddly iddly.
> How would you like to be me?

For years my honorary Auntie Evelyn and Uncle Mac lived in

the former stables in the park. Uncle Mac was then the deputy head of Liverpool's parks and gardens and a Royal Horticultural Society judge. At the time Liverpool had an amazing collection of orchids in the hothouses at Calderstones Park. He taught me to appreciate them, even the brown ones that, at first, I took against because of their colour. Japanese garden design was another of his enthusiasms and he established a Japanese garden in the park.

Auntie Evelyn and Uncle Mac's own Calderstones garden contained a large swing. Their daughter, Janet, and I would spend hours on it, trying to get higher and higher so we could peep into the walled garden on the other side of their boundary wall. The walled garden was the place to feed birds – sparrows, bluetits, robins and chaffinches; but children were only allowed in it in the company of an adult. It was not a secret garden but a forbidden garden, and that was part of its attraction.

When Uncle Mac was promoted to become head of Liverpool's parks and gardens, his family moved to a big pseudo-Elizabethan house in Ibbotsons Lane on the edge of Sefton Park. The house was a very impressive tied cottage as, like the stables house in Calderstones Park, it was owned by Liverpool Corporation. Sefton Park is vast, covering 235 acres. It contains a large lake, a Peter Pan statue, a Fairy Glen, a cave and a big Victorian palm house; but mostly when I went there I was content just to admire Auntie Evelyn and Uncle Mac's garden. It fell steeply down to a stream, was full of plants and incredibly peaceful.

After he became Town Clerk, my father developed an interesting connection with Sefton Park. Each year he accompanied members of the city's Consular Corps to a ceremony at the palm house in the park. In those days, thanks to its long historical connection with shipping, the city still had a large Consular Corps of about twenty-six members. Some of these were honorary consuls, but some worked full time. The consuls gave support to Liverpool residents from their own country and to their country's visiting seafarers.

During the annual palm house ceremony a wreath was laid at the foot of a statue of Simón Bolívar, the South American revolutionary who was instrumental in freeing Bolivia, Colombia, Ecuador and Venezuela from Spanish colonialism. I found it strange when I heard that among the statues taken away from the palm house, in the midst of the Labour left-wing control of the City Council, was the statue of Simón Bolívar. I find it even stranger that now nobody seems to be able to tell me where his statue has gone.

Sefton Park and Calderstones Park are two of a number of parks in south Liverpool. The only other park I cared about as a child was Woolton Woods. There I would stand for a long time waiting for the floral cuckoo clock to say 'cuckoo'. I could never work out where the cuckoo mechanism was located. Was it up in a tree? Was it in a gardener's hut? Nobody ever told me.

Another green space, Wavertree Mystery, was not really a park, but a vast open field of over a hundred acres. Sometimes it was called Wavertree Playground. Responsibility for its upkeep was part of my honorary Uncle Mac's department. It was called The Mystery because nobody locally knew who had gifted it to the City Council. What we did know was that a condition of the gift was that it should be 'kept as an open space forever'.

Holy Trinity Wavertree church and the Liverpool Blue Coat School overlooked The Mystery. It was a good place for local children to play rounders and other ball games, but it came into its own each year when the Liverpool Show was held on it. Sadly the show was abolished in the early 1970s, but when I was growing up it was in its heyday. It was held in the school summer holidays, so children could attend every one of its three days.

My most exciting visits to the showground took place the night before the show opened to the public. My father always took me with him when he went to check on how the preparations were going. By then the large show ring had been marked out and steeply tiered wooden seating, with a canvas awning above it, erected at one side. During the evening, cattle trucks arrived from Cheshire and north Wales and headed for a large tent near the already marked-out cattle ring.

On the eve of the show's opening, floral and vegetable displays were being set up in the huge floral marquee and the scent of flowers filled the air. I particularly looked forward to the next day when I could read the very waspish comments the judges of the flower arrangement section had written on the judging cards placed by each arrangement. The judges did not pull their punches and, at times, seemed to be quite rude.

I was in awe of the vast displays arranged by flower and vegetable growers and local authorities. Southport's floral display always seemed to me to be the best; but my uncle told me that, apart from Liverpool's, he thought Swansea had the best local authority parks in Britain.

The night before the show, some of the tents and show rings were still being erected. My father only relaxed when he saw that preparations were well in hand. Just before we went home, we always called in at a green painted wooden pavilion standing next to the roadway in the middle of The Mystery. It served as the show's office. Inside we would always find Uncle Mac busy making final arrangements for the next day's opening.

In retrospect I can see that my parents sometimes had problems with my being at the Liverpool Show. They needed to attend formal events – lunches, opening ceremonies, prize awards, etc. – at which my presence would have been a nuisance. Sometimes, to my delight, Bessie Braddock MP would look after me. Once my parents were so desperate for childcare they asked a boy called David Hunt to look after me. I was furious because he was only a year older than me and, even worse, he was a boy. David later served as an MP for the Wirral between 1976 and 1997, and eventually became Lord Hunt of Wirral.

However, my parents' main solution to the problem of my

presence at the show was to deposit me in the show Chairman's roped-off special section of the grandstand, overlooking the main show ring. The steward in charge of admission to that section was regularly asked to keep an eye on me.

From my perch, high up in the grandstand, I watched some of the best showjumpers of the time, as well as the Liverpool police horses performing their traditional musical ride. Each year my mother judged the best decorated horse competition at the show. Before she made her choice the decorated horses were paraded around the main show ring; they were all carthorses.

In the early 1950s carthorses were still sometimes used to pull bin carts round the streets of the city. The binmen took great pride in decorating their horses with flowers made out of crêpe paper, and in polishing the horse brasses so they gleamed in the sun. My mother looked very small as she stood in the ring in front of those huge horses and presented rosettes to the winners. Today a memorial statue of a Liverpool carthorse has been placed near the Museum of Liverpool by the Pier Head. Standing next to it, I can imagine my mother proudly attaching a red rosette to the horse's bridle.

I was perfectly safe on my own in the show Chairman's special section of the grandstand; but my mother got very flustered the day she arrived to collect me from it and found me chatting to a dapper gentleman with gap teeth, a moustache and a carnation in his buttonhole. It was the comedy actor and film star Terry Thomas who was visiting the show to judge the Miss Liverpool beauty competition. My mother certainly did not want her little girl to talk to him. Carried away by his filming roles, she said he was 'a spiv'.

My mother was most unenthusiastic about the annual Miss Liverpool beauty competition. If she had known the word, she would have described the competition as sexist. However, she felt she had to accompany my father to it.

The only time I remember going with my parents to the Miss Liverpool competition, my mother again got very flustered. On that occasion the judges were the comedians Jimmy Jewel and Ben Warriss. Before the competition opened, the comedians turned round in their seats and started to talk to me. They were very kind and suggested that I should move from my seat next to my parents in the second row, and sit next to them in the front row. From there, they said, I would have a better view of the women in their glad rags and bathing costumes. My mother was not having that. She knew the sort of jokes the two comedians might make at a beauty competition, and they were not the sort of jokes she liked her daughter to hear.

My mother was even disapproving of the thought of my presence in the jazz tent at the show. Consequently, I missed out on hearing Acker Bilk, the Merseysippi Jazz Band and George Melly. Fortunately, she had no reservations about my showing my pet rabbit – Frisky Silky Bobbety Bun Rabbit Holmes, or just Bun for short – at the show. Bun was a black and white rabbit with black spots on his side and a black stripe down his back. He had been born in a backyard in Wavertree with too few spots to be shown by a breeder and, until we saved him, had been destined for the pot.

I arrived early at the show that year clutching a box containing my pet. The rabbit tent was large. There were already a lot of rabbits in single hutches placed on trestle tables forming an oblong around the edges of the tent. In the middle of the oblong there were a few more tables; that was where I was told to take my boxed rabbit first.

Hesitantly I approached the central table. Bun was immediately taken from me: grabbed by his ears in a degrading manner. 'Huh' sneered a man standing nearby. 'That rabbit will never win. It's the skinniest rabbit in the whole of the north-west of England.'

I was near to tears. How could he say that? My friends, Doreen and Mary, and I regularly fed Bun with dandelions, picked from the grass verges on our way home from school and in the school holidays. We worried a bit about that. Somebody had told us that if you picked dandelions you would wet your knickers; but we had been told that dandelions were good for rabbits, so we were not deterred. We loved Bun too much for that.

We loved Bun so much that sometimes, on wet days, we carried him into the house to play. There we sat on the green carpet in the hall eating sandwiches and pretending that, as we had a rabbit for company, we were really sitting among the hills of the Clwydian range. We imagined we were in the sun at the top of Moel Famau in Wales. Bun seemed to enjoy such days. He made zizzing noises of pleasure to show how much he appreciated our company.

The dandelions we collected were added to oats, carrots, lettuce and tea leaves, just like the rabbit breeder had recommended. Bun, I believed, was a very fit rabbit. But that year, as I left the show tent, I began to worry that maybe the sneering man was right after all. Perhaps Bun would not win anything, and perhaps he was indeed the skinniest rabbit in the whole of the north-west of England.

Later that day I returned to the rabbit tent in trepidation. The trestle tables stretched for yards. On top of them, in hutch after hutch, exceedingly fat rabbits of assorted colours contentedly slept the day away. Only at the far end of the tent was something happening. There a line of muttering people stood with bits of grass in their hands. They were queuing up intent on feeding the one non-somnolent rabbit in the whole of the Liverpool Show.

As I walked towards the queue the muttering grew louder: 'Terrible.' 'Cruel.' 'It's so thin.' 'The owner must starve it.' 'Look, it's even eaten its prize certificate.'

My Bun had never known so much delightful and generous company. He was zizzing with pleasure and enthusiastically keeping up with the food supply. I walked closer. The sneering man had been wrong. Bun had won a Commended certificate, and found its edges very edible. Slipping under the grass-proffering hands to rescue what was left of that card, I did not know whether to be proud or embarrassed.

Dear Bessie Braddock

HER STATUE STANDS at Lime Street Station – Bessie Braddock, the Labour MP for Liverpool Exchange constituency from 1945 to 1970. In her time Bessie was an unusual figure: a widely loved politician.

It is odd to see bronze statues of people you once knew in the flesh. For example, the statue of Harold Wilson outside Huddersfield railway station is in many ways excellent. It is Harold to the life, except in one respect – there is no pipe. The former Prime Minster and MP for Huyton always had his pipe with him when he was in public. Puffing on it enabled him to pause and think during conversations. I suspect the pipe has been omitted for reasons of political correctness, but it does not look right to me.

I feel a similar unease when looking at Bessie in bronze. Though the top conveys her ample bosom, the real Bessie was, as I recall, somewhat broader on the beam. The statue has, however, got the real Bessie's hat, handbag and feeling of bustling along just right. Before Mrs Thatcher carried her handbag round British politics, Bessie had her handbag. Indeed, as the statue shows, she was often to be seen with two bags, the other being her briefcase.

I first became acquainted with Bessie's handbag when I was seven, and she was at the Liverpool Show. She attended that annual city event with enthusiasm. On the day I first remember meeting her, Bessie, my mother and I were in the tented ladies' lavatory at the side of the show Chairman's tent. Inside the actual tent, civic dignitaries and distinguished guests were assembling for a formal lunch complete with speeches. As part of the ceremony I was supposed to present the Lady Mayoress with a bouquet; but I was refusing to do so on political grounds.

Bessie and my mother were working together on breaking down my resistance.

The background to this incident involved the religious differences that were so intense in the city sixty years ago. In 1950 the Conservative party had been in danger of losing control of Liverpool City Council. To keep themselves in power they did a deal with the Liverpool Protestant Party and installed its leader, Alderman Reverend Harry Longbottom, as Lord Mayor. If they had not done so, they would not have kept their control of the City Council; they needed his casting vote.

Soon after Alderman Longbottom's installation as Lord Mayor, the annual civic service was held at the church where he served as the minister. My parents attended the service. By then I was used to my mother attending civic events and returning without saying much about what she had been doing. This time things were different. She seemed very upset by that church service.

The Liverpool Protestant Party was founded on hatred of other Christians: that is, on hatred of Roman Catholics. This hatred between two denominations of the same religion was, in those days, as extreme in parts of Liverpool as it was in Northern Ireland and Glasgow. My mother knew that. She expected Orange Lodge members to attend the civic service in droves, and they did; after all, the election of the Protestant Party's leader as the city's first citizen was a victory for them. But what had really upset her were the hymns sung in the church. They were, she said, 'Hymns of hate'.

I was interested to find out what constituted a hymn of hate. I found an Order of Service lying around in our house. I proceeded to read it and concluded my mother was right: Alderman Longbottom's church sang in praise of hatred of other Christians. In my childlike way, I reasoned that as hate was bad, Alderman Longbottom was bad. If Alderman Longbottom was bad, his wife, Mrs Longbottom, was also bad.

The Lady Mayoress I was supposed to present a bouquet to at

the Liverpool Show that year was, of course, Mrs Longbottom. Because her husband's church sang hymns of hate, I refused to present her with the bouquet. In the tented ladies' lavatory at the show, my mother tried to cajole me to change my mind. But I was adamant: I was not going to give a bouquet to a bad lady. Eventually Bessie found the answer to my intransigence. Out of her handbag she pulled a sweet. Would I present the bouquet if she gave me a sweet? I would.

Bessie had bribed me for the sake of the city's image. The bouquet was duly presented, and a photograph of the Lady Mayoress bending forward to receive it taken for the record. In my defence I would say that sweet rationing, introduced during the war, was still in force in 1950. It did not end until 1953, so the offer of a sweet was a rare treat.

Bessie went to the Liverpool Show in her role as an MP. Her husband, Jack Braddock, was on the City Council and served as its leader between 1955 and 1961. Sometimes at the show he needed to attend events my parents also attended, while Bessie was left free to do other things. I loved it when Bessie took me along to some of the other things; but found sitting next to her watching the so-called 'Morris Dancing' extremely boring.

This dancing consisted of assorted teams of girls, dressed as majorettes with very short skirts and twirling batons, dancing by raising their white socked, plimsoll-clad feet in time to music. I soon got bored. After a time the teams began to look alike to me, despite the varied colours of their uniforms and batons.

The most boring aspect of the dancing was the music. It seemed to me that only three tunes came over the loudspeakers. I was watching the same routines performed to the same music for what seemed hours and hours. Worse still, Bessie and I were sitting in the VIP area. We were in the front row facing the dancers and in full view of the crowd of proud parents and grandparents. I did not dare to wriggle, even a tiny bit.

Eventually I whispered my boredom to Bessie. She told me off in no uncertain terms. I was a very lucky girl. I had a nice house and loving parents. Here I was sitting watching children who did not have my advantages. One or both of these children's parents might not be around. Their father might have been killed in the war. They did not have many toys, and their homes were not as nice as mine. They deserved my full attention. I should count myself lucky, sit still and watch with an appreciative smile. That would be good for me too. When I grew up I might marry an ambassador or an MP, then I would have to sit for hours watching even more boring things with a smile on my face.

That was an interesting comment from Bessie. She was a national figure and a popular high-profile MP. Her husband Jack was only known locally, being the Labour Party's leader on the City Council, but he was the dominant figure in their marriage. Years later, I did marry an MP and recalled my telling-off that day with amusement. Bessie, I thought, had been prescient.

Bessie, like many people in Liverpool, was very conscious of the gulf which existed between rich and poor in the city. One of the ways in which she sought to enable poor children to rise from poverty was in her support for boxing clubs. I found her advocacy of people hitting each other difficult to understand. How, I wondered, could such a gentle and loving person as Bessie encourage people to hurt each other? Not only that, how could she encourage people to watch other people hurting each other?

When it came to ideas, Bessie treated children's views seriously. Unlike many adults at the time, she did not talk down to me. Instead she explained that people who lived in Liverpool's slums could only escape from them if they got money. One of the ways to get money was to become a famous boxer. The Liverpool singer, the late Frankie Vaughan, started his career in boxing before being recognised for his singing. Liverpool boxing clubs gave boys something to do in parts of the city where there was little available to them, apart from a life of poverty or crime.

It was such a pity that Bessie and Jack Braddock did not have children, though they seemed very proud of a niece about whom Bessie talked often. She delighted in being with children, and always seemed to know what would interest them. One day I was sitting next to her at a circus. It was a traditional, and now not politically correct, circus complete with horses, lions, tigers and elephants. We were sitting in the front row with the metal animal cage and the red-coated ringmaster cracking his whip only feet away.

That was exciting enough, but my evening was topped after the show when Bessie asked me if I would like to go with her to meet the circus owners. She knew them well, which is why she was able to take me into one of their caravans. I was overwhelmed. The caravan was like a grotto with shining ornaments everywhere, and all so neat and tidy; to think that all this travelled from town to town and next year would be back in the park.

Jack and Bessie Braddock were a very close couple. They were united in their politics, travelling from early membership of the Communist Party to what was described by commentators as right-wing Labour. But the city of Liverpool and the welfare of its inhabitants were of overwhelming importance to both of them.

Although the Braddocks were members of the Labour Party, they had friends across all parties and in all walks of life. These friends included Sir John Moores, who was a Conservative and owner of Littlewoods Football Pools and shops. The Braddocks recognised that the exhibitions of modern art, sponsored by Sir John, were good for the city, even though they may have had reservations about the style of some of the art on display.

When Jack Braddock had a heart attack and died at an event to celebrate the opening of a John Moores exhibition at the Walker Art Gallery, my parents were very concerned for Bessie. They wondered how she would be able to carry on with her political life, for they knew how much she depended on her husband's support. She might give the impression of being a battling virago, but in fact she was a softie at heart. The shock of Jack's death did affect Bessie greatly, but she continued in politics and was deputy chairman of the Labour Party in 1968, just two years before her death.

By the mid-1960s I had become a national official of the Labour Party, serving as Local Government Officer at that party's headquarters in Smith Square, Westminster. I saw Bessie regularly at Labour Party events. Checking in to the Imperial Hotel, Blackpool, for one of Labour's annual conferences, she stressed to me the importance of finding out the location of the fire exits the moment I got to my bedroom. To this day I still follow her advice.

At one Labour Party annual conference, Bessie asked me to write her a background note on the then Labour Government's housing policy. She was to reply to a debate on housing from the platform on behalf of the party's National Executive Committee. Given Liverpool's housing problems, this would be a particularly important speech. Alas I had not realised that, by then, Bessie was beginning to suffer from dementia and was finding concentration difficult. What she needed from me was very different from what she actually asked for. She needed me to write her speech for her; but, instead of asking for a speech, she had asked for a background note.

My first job after graduating from the London School of Economics had been as a research assistant on demographic (population) statistics to a sociologist called Ralph Miliband, whose two sons, Ed and David, became Labour MPs. Statistics in those days were not in as common use as they are today. Computers have made statistics a matter of everyday conversation. But, in the early-1960s, there were no home computers and things like pie and bar charts, that are now taught in junior schools, were often not taught until people went to university.

Nevertheless, working for the Labour Party fifty years ago and having earlier worked as a demographer, I tended to assume that politicians were as fascinated by statistics as

I was. I thought all politicians could understand them and that they found statistics useful. Consequently, within Bessie's background housing note, I included a table showing how well Harold Wilson's Government claimed it had done in building new homes.

On the day of the debate, I stood at the back of the conference hall and listened as Bessie read out my background note word for word as if it were her speech, including a reference: 'See the table on page...'

I had not realised how rapidly Bessie's brain was deteriorating. When she had asked me for that background note she had seemed quite lucid.

Mental deterioration in the elderly was not a subject people talked about openly in those days. Shortly before Bessie died, I got on the same 77 bus in London as she did. We were both on the top deck. The bus was heading from Euston station to Westminster. I said 'Hello' to her, but Bessie did not recognise me. I was devastated. Looking back, she was obviously suffering from dementia, whether from Alzheimer's or a series of mini strokes. She died soon after, in 1970. A short time beforehand, she and her friend Sir John Moores had both been granted the Freedom of the City of Liverpool, an honour they both greatly deserved.

Bessie loved flowers. She grew her own freesias at a time when those flowers were rarely seen. Now freesia bulbs and flowers can be bought in many places. When I buy them I think fondly of her. She was a great woman. Not for our Bessie moans about male discrimination against women in politics; not for her calls for positive discrimination in favour of women. Like other women politicians of her generation, she did not have time for that sort of thing; she was too busy battling on behalf of all the people living in her dear city.

Oh, the squalor of it all

SLIMY WAS THE word to describe the walls leading upstairs to my auntie's flat in Windsor Street, Liverpool 8. Even the walls inside the flat seemed sticky. The place smelt of dirt and sweat. There seemed to be bugs living in the walls. Following my parents up the stairs, I felt scared.

My auntie's flat was above a pawnbroker's shop. In the 1940s hard-up families regularly pawned almost everything they had, including clothes. I did not know it at the time, being only five years old, but the smell was probably coming through the floorboards and emanated from the pawned goods in the shop below the flat.

Windsor Street is in Toxteth, an area that was then infested with cockroaches and vermin. The street is quite near the docks and river; consequently there were quite a few rats scuttling round the streets. In my auntie's flat even the small brown beetles I saw running around made me cringe.

As a baby I was christened nearby at St Michael-in-the-Hamlet Church, Toxteth. The church is listed Grade One and is known as the 'Cast Iron Church' because it is built of cast iron. It is near the stretch of Mersey riverbank called the Cast Iron Shore, which is also known as locally as 'The Cazzy'. I have never returned to that church and I am grateful that, unlike some of my cousins, I never lived in Toxteth.

My auntie and her family felt very differently. They considered themselves lucky to be living in the Toxteth flat. Sadly they were right to feel lucky. Housing conditions in

Liverpool had been bad for many people even before the Second World War. There were lots of overcrowded squalid slums in the city even then. During the Second World War, German bombs demolished or damaged many homes, making people homeless. This increased the need for families to share accommodation with others.

By the time the bombing stopped, crumbling walls and strewn bricks could be seen everywhere downtown and in the inner suburbs. Moreover, the shortage of building materials meant that even homes undamaged by bombing could not be maintained. For many Liverpool people, including some members of my family, housing conditions after the war were atrocious.

My auntie had only been able to rent the flat above the pawnbroker's shop thanks to the kindness of her older sister's friend who was a schoolteacher and married to the owner of the building. This lady, who naturally became my honorary Auntie Marjorie, had taken pity on my real auntie, who was unwell and about to be homeless.

Auntie Marjorie was not the only one to help the family. Standing in that gloomy flat one day, I saw two Roman Catholic nursing nuns leaning over my real auntie's bed. It did not matter to them that my auntie was a Protestant. The nuns were there to help the poor of the city whatever their religion. I asked my mother what was wrong with my auntie, and was told she was 'away with the fairies' and had had a baby. In those days knowledge of mental illness was scant and the medications available very limited.

Some time after that visit to Windsor Street, the Corporation rehoused my auntie's family. As part of the removal process, all their property was taken to a council depot in Smithdown Road to be fumigated. While that was being done, one of my cousins came to stay with us briefly. She had only been in the house about half an hour, when I heard my grandmother marching her along the corridor to the bathroom saying loudly 'Nits' and 'Carbolic'. A metal comb, carbolic soap and hot water were produced, and my cousin and grandmother were in the bathroom a very long time.

I find it odd that, today, there is a tendency for parents whose children have nits to assert that nits only like clean hair. Nits just like hair. Liverpool's overcrowded slums provided ideal conditions for nits to spread from child's head to child's head. In school in the 1950s, a visiting nurse regularly inspected our hair. She was popularly called the Nit Nurse. We expected the Nit Nurse's regular visits just as we expected, if we were off school sick, somebody from the council's Education Department to call at our house to check we were really ill and not playing truant.

My Auntie Fran, teaching in downtown Liverpool between the wars, once told a mother that her child had nits. The parental retort was instant: 'So what. He's got nits. Everybody's got nits. You've got nits. I've got nits. The Queen's got nits.'

After the Second World War councillors and officials in Liverpool felt overwhelmed by people's housing needs. They tried to solve the city's slum problems by enthusiastic house building. Unfortunately, they were in some ways too enthusiastic. They rehoused people in unsuitable accommodation. They built homes of such poor quality that, only a few decades later, the new homes were demolished.

My auntie's family's rehousing from Liverpool 8 was an example of how it is possible to have the best intentions, but get things very wrong. Initially, the family were delighted with their new flat at The Green near Broadgreen Hospital, but within weeks the problems started.

It was not a good idea to put three young children on the top floor of a three-storey block that had steps going down from the street to the block's entrance and no lift. Prams can be heavy, and flights of stairs or steps are always a challenge for mothers with young children. There was also the problem of soundproofing – or rather lack of soundproofing. So inadequate was this that the people on the floor below my auntie were constantly complaining. They made their disapproval of my cousins' noise known by banging on their ceiling with a broom handle.

In 1963 I saw, from within the city's Housing Department, just how bad was Liverpool's housing stock. I also saw how the City Council, in its enthusiasm to knock down slums and build new dwellings, had still not got the right balance between the number of new homes they built and the quality of what they built.

As a sociology undergraduate at the London School of Economics, I was required to write a mini-thesis. Graeme Shankland, planning consultant to the City Council at the time, offered me the opportunity to work with him on aspects of Liverpool's planning. When I got to the office, I was unhappy with what he wanted me to do. He was kind to offer, but I really could not face undertaking a feasibility study for the construction of a tower block of flats at the Pier Head, south of what are now called The Three Graces. In those days the Graces were more mundanely known as the Cunard Building, the Liver Building and the Mersey Dock and Harbour Board Offices.

Rejecting Graeme Shankland's offer, I arranged instead to study the way the city's Housing Department operated. That summer I visited many people working in the department. I accompanied some of them as they went around the city. I visited downtown slums as well as, supposedly wonderful, new tower blocks in the suburbs.

I will never forget accompanying a housing officer who was issuing closure notices in the slums near the Collegiate School in Shaw Street. One family I met lived in a single room. They were a married couple with two teenage sons. In the room there were two double beds with the dirtiest sheets I have ever seen, plus a small tatty table. That was all. The woman told us she cooked at the grate. The water tap out the back and the outside privy were shared with other families. No wonder the sheets were so filthy. There was nowhere to wash and dry them. The same applied to clothes.

Photographs can give an impression of the broken walls, clouded windows, dirt and poverty that then existed in Liverpool's slums. Fortunately nobody wants to reproduce the smells that all too often wafted through the air. It was not the people's fault. They tried to be clean. But when men could get work it was gruelling and often filthy, and they brought the dirt home with them on their clothes and bodies.

When people arrived home from work, many did not have the facilities to wash themselves and their clothes properly. True, after Kitty Wilkinson opened England's first public wash house in 1842, Liverpool slowly developed a network of public wash houses in which both people and their clothes could be washed; and, in the middle of last century, there were still quite a few public wash houses open in the city. However, using them took time and involved spending money families often did not have.

Some uncharitable and bigoted Protestants, in those days, would assert that Catholics were smelly. This was in part a reflection of the silly hatred that then existed in parts of the city between two forms of Christianity. Sadly it was also, to some extent, a reflection of reality.

The Roman Catholic Irish were among the most recent immigrants to the city and so had the worst choice of accommodation. Often such families had a religious opposition to birth control and this meant many had large families. Consequently, many of the city's poorest families were Roman Catholics. They tended to live in the poorest housing, to be the most overcrowded and to undertake the dirtiest manual labour. With less access to water, they and their clothes were washed less often than the clothes and bodies of their better-off fellow citizens, who would have done well not to comment.

The Roman Catholic/Protestant divide in the city affected housing allocations. Protestants wanted to live near Protestants, and Roman Catholics wanted to live near Roman Catholics. Interviewing an official responsible for housing allocations for families being rehoused under slum clearance schemes, I asked how he dealt with this sectarian problem. His solution was simple. Families were entitled to three offers of accommodation. These had to be different sorts of offers. He was not allowed to offer a family a flat too near to one they had already rejected.

As an example of how things worked, the official cited some new flats on the Scotland Road, which was known locally as 'the Scottie'. If he first offered a Roman Catholic family a flat on the Protestant side of the Scottie they would turn it down. He would then have to offer them a flat on the other side of the road – on the Catholic side. This meant delay in rehousing the family.

It saved him and the family time, and the City Council money, if the first offer he made to a Catholic family was on the Catholic side of the Scottie and not on the Protestant side. Similarly, it made sense if the first offer he made to a Protestant family was on the Protestant side of the road, and not on the Catholic side. Consequently that was what he did.

The same Housing Department official noted with amusement that on St Patrick's Day in March, one side of the Scottie was festooned with green; and, on the Glorious Twelfth of July, the other side was festooned with orange.

It never occurred to me to ask that official how he knew which families were Roman Catholic and which were Protestant. I know that, at the time, patients admitted to Liverpool hospitals were asked their religion, and that that information was included on a card displayed at the side of their hospital locker. Perhaps the Housing Department's forms asked for similar information.

The family living in a single room in Shaw Street near the Collegiate School, and on whom the other housing officer issued a closure order, were as delighted as my auntie had been at the prospect of Liverpool Corporation rehousing them. They were told they would be moved to Kirkby, a vast new housing estate on the edge of the city.

As he filled in his form, the housing officer talked to the family about furniture. They did not have any furniture, apart from the two beds and small rickety table. Those items took up all the available space in their room; but the man said they would buy some furniture on hire purchase when they were moved. The officer noted that fact on the form.

Hire purchase was a relatively new concept at the time and was used by many families when they were rehoused. Like payday loans today, it seemed an easy solution to an immediate problem, but could put a huge strain on a family's budget. Added to this particular financial strain were other pressures associated with rehousing.

There was not much employment available in the housing developments at Kirkby. Men who had worked in the docks or in the warehouses on the Dock Road did not usually own cars, so after they moved to Kirkby, they had to pay bus fares to travel into town if they wanted to continue working there. Previously they had probably walked to work. On top of the bus fares, rehousing placed other new burdens on family budgets. There were rates to pay and rents were usually considerably higher than in the slums. Food and clothing away from the city centre markets and corner shops were more expensive.

Before I visited Kirkby as part of my undergraduate studies, I was shown the City Council's plan for the area. The plan had quite a few splashes of green. I asked when the proposed parks and other community facilities the green splashes on the plan represented were going to be built.

It was explained to me that much of that sort of thing would have to wait. The green splashes were extras. They were to be the icing on the cake. The overwhelming task was to move people from bombed homes and squalid slums into new homes. Families needed modern conveniences like bathrooms and kitchens of their own. Only when the slums had been cleared and overcrowding ended, would proper attention then be given to communal luxuries like parks and playgrounds.

In the meantime, the green splashes on the plan represented unloved and undeveloped vacant land.

This was all very well intentioned, but visiting the Kirkby housing office I saw the effects of uprooting families from the inner city. The parents loved the new clean kitchens and bathrooms, but the children had nowhere safe to play out. They missed friends and family living nearby and offering friendship and support during family emergencies. Bits of building materials left on the vacant land proved attractive to bored children, who were tempted to use them as destructive missiles against each other and against the new buildings.

After moving to Kirkby, a lot of people became miserable and financially overstretched. The new environment might be healthier physically, but mental health problems seemed to increase.

That summer of 1963, as I listened to people who had been happy to be rehoused but had then become unhappy, it became clear to me that the City Council's enthusiasm for building tower blocks of flats was developing into a major problem. The council, like many local authorities at the time, had become obsessed by concrete. Industrialised building methods (shortened to IB) were being promoted by central government as being quicker than conventional methods of building.

For a city with such a terrible housing problem, IB seemed to be the answer. As the slums were knocked down, concrete tower blocks – many now demolished in their turn – were put up all over the city. So proud were councillors, of all political persuasions, of these now demolished edifices that blocks were often named after members of the City Council. Examples included The Braddocks, named after Labour's Bessie and Jack Braddock, and Entwistle Heights, named after the Conservative Leader of the City Council between 1961 and 1963, Sir Maxwell Entwistle.

Local authorities throughout the country took against the building of tower blocks, and naming them after councillors, following a gas explosion in 1968 at the 22-storey Ronan Point in east London. In that explosion four people were killed and many others injured. At the time, some of his fellow councillors on the London borough of Newham Council told me they thought Alderman Ronan, after whom the block had been named, would never recover from the sadness he felt. He had tried to improve people's lives by building new homes, but his surname would forever be associated with tragedy.

After the war, intent on clearing the slums, local councillors took great pride in seeing huge lead weights, hanging from cranes, being swung against rows of terraced slum houses. One day, Sir Keith Joseph MP, who was Minister of Housing and Local Government between 1962 and 1964, visited Liverpool. A slum-smashing demonstration, complete with audience of councillors, aldermen and council officials was laid on especially for the Minister.

Just as the crane swung its weight towards the brick terrace, two workmen jumped out from a ground-floor window. It was a good job they did so; the organisers of the ceremony had forgotten about the workmen. They could have been killed.

Nearly two years after my undergraduate study of Liverpool's Housing Department, I was working in London at the Labour Party's headquarters. I was that party's researcher on housing policy. An academic at the London School of Economics told me research showed that if only the building industry, and particularly building suppliers, could get its act together it would be just as easy and cost effective to build by conventional methods as by IB.

Horrified by what I had seen in Liverpool, I tried to dissuade Dick Crossman MP, who then was Minister of Housing and Local Government, from promoting IB. I was wasting my time. His Minister of State, Bob Mellish MP, like so many politicians at the time, was completely sold on pre-cast concrete, and Dick was not really interested.

People who are not from Liverpool and who have never seen, felt or smelt its slums, cannot understand the searing effect the knowledge of their existence had on many Liverpudlians.

Compassion for fellow human beings living, growing up, and dying in squalor prompted people to feel they needed to do something. So much poverty, and what would now be called disadvantage, in one place is hard to take without feeling the need to act.

Neil Kinnock, the Labour Party's leader between 1983 and 1992, seemed not to understand this when, at Bournemouth in 1985, he singled out the city for attack in a keynote speech to Labour's annual conference. He was right to say that the City Council had behaved irresponsibly at the time. By spending so much money on housing and other services it had bankrupted itself. It had also carried out acts of municipal vandalism. However, I felt the Labour Party nationally should have done something much earlier to sort out its Liverpool organisation, instead of pillorying the whole city after so much damage had been done by Labour's own members.

The then Labour MP for Liverpool Walton, Eric Heffer, was so upset with Neil Kinnock's speech at that Bournemouth conference, he walked off the platform in a huff. Seated at the back of that hall, I slipped out quietly and sat on Bournemouth's pier with tears streaming down my face. Growing up in the south Wales valleys and accompanying his mother on her nursing rounds, Neil Kinnock must have seen poverty, but on a much smaller scale to the Liverpool slums. He simply did not understand; perhaps it was too much to expect him to understand.

The Little House

Was it a message from God or merely coincidence? My father was not sure, but it was certainly very odd.

One day, in Dr Kitty Frazer's waiting room at Tuebrook, he picked up a short tract from a rack on the mantelpiece above the gas fire. It talked about the good works a Miss Constance Davidson was doing among deprived boys in Wavertree village, Liverpool. Next day, on his office desk, my father found a letter, addressed to the Town Clerk's Department, from the same Miss Davidson. In the letter she asked for financial support for her work.

In the 1950s deprived children were not described as disadvantaged. They were simply poor, and some were very poor. Public sector grants to charities scarcely existed then. The terms 'social entrepreneur' and 'social enterprise' had not been invented. Miss Davidson was, therefore, most unlikely to get any help for her work from Liverpool's ratepayers. Most people at that time would have said she was wasting her time writing a begging letter to the Town Clerk's Department. However, my father was fascinated by this juxtaposition of events, and decided to undertake a personal investigation. With my mother, he called on Miss Davidson at her home in Wavertree High Street.

Miss Davidson's background was interesting. She was from a well-off Scottish family. They were Protestants and her brother had been a Moderator of the Church of Scotland; but she had become a Roman Catholic. Feeling burdened by her wealth, she decided to devote her life to helping the poor. She started doing this by giving away most of her money and living among the poor in a Glasgow slum.

Never having done any housework in her life, Miss Davidson

introduced herself to her new Glasgow neighbours by throwing a whole bucket of hot water down the tenement's staircase in an attempt to clean it. Unfortunately she did not have a mop. That did not make her neighbours happy. It was perhaps a good thing then that, soon afterwards, she was told Liverpool's slums were worse than Glasgow's, and believed God was telling her to move on.

After arriving in Liverpool, Miss Davidson began to live in The Little House, Wavertree High Street. The Little House really was a little house. From the front door, a small passageway led into the back parlour where a fire often burned in a small black range. Two wooden chairs stood by the fire. A doorway led from the parlour into a dining room in which the only furniture was a long table and a lot of dining chairs. The dining room's tiny window looked out on to the High Street. There was also a small kitchen leading off the back parlour and beyond that a yard with an outside privy.

There were two bedrooms upstairs. They were reached by opening what looked like a cupboard door in the parlour and climbing up a narrow staircase. The front bedroom was full of bunk beds. The smaller back room, on to which the staircase opened, was almost empty. All it contained was a wooden armchair and a prie-dieu, at which Miss Davidson spent some time each day on her knees praying.

Miss Davidson explained to my parents that she took in, and cared for, boys whose parents either did not want them, or could not cope with them. Such was the poverty in Wavertree village at the time that she had lots of requests for her services. It was soon after the war when rationing was still in force, so a ration book was handed over to Miss Davidson whenever a boy went to live at The Little House.

She only took in boys who agreed to go to church regularly, and who were either already baptised or whose parents agreed to their son's baptism. Though she was a Roman Catholic, she did not mind if the boys were baptised into the Church of England, provided that was their parents' denomination.

Grandad Holmes – not the stature for a docker.

Grandma Holmes.

My father as a child.

Grandma and Grandad Burton.

My mother, aged six.

My mother celebrating St David's Day in Liverpool.

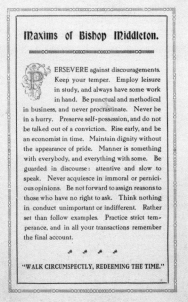

LIVERPOOL COLLEGIATE SCHOOL,
SHAW STREET.

In remembrance of your old School, will you fasten this card in your desk or on the wall of your bedroom and look at it sometimes. It is not intended that the reading of this card should replace your reading the Bible, where you learn the greater lesson— "to help others."

You are now going out from School into the wider world. Bear in mind the Englishman's motto—"RUN STRAIGHT."

You have the best wishes of all your masters for your welfare.

S. E. Brown.

Maxims of Bishop Middleton.

PERSEVERE against discouragements. Keep your temper. Employ leisure in study, and always have some work in hand. Be punctual and methodical in business, and never procrastinate. Never be in a hurry. Preserve self-possession, and do not be talked out of a conviction. Rise early, and be an economist in time. Maintain dignity without the appearance of pride. Manner is something with everybody, and everything with some. Be guarded in discourse: attentive and slow to speak. Never acquiesce in immoral or pernicious opinions. Be not forward to assign reasons to those who have no right to ask. Think nothing in conduct unimportant or indifferent. Rather set than follow examples. Practice strict temperance, and in all your transactions remember the final account.

"WALK CIRCUMSPECTLY, REDEEMING THE TIME."

The front and back of a card posted to my father after he left the Collegiate School.

My parents' wedding, with bridesmaid (Auntie Dorothy) and best man (Uncle Ronnie).

With my mother at 60 Muirhead Avenue.

My father in ornate Town Clerk's robes.

Officers of St Christopher's Norris Green Life Boys.

St Christopher's Norris Green Life Boys on Moel Famau in the early-1930s. Health and safety fears seem to have been nonexistent.

My parents at Life Boys camp.

Penny Lane roundabout, October 1956. Heathfield Road Welsh Chapel can be seen rear left behind the parked buses. The Trustee Savings Bank, with clock above door is at rear right.

Penny Lane roundabout in 2016, with the Welsh Chapel demolished and an extra storey being added to the former waiting room and lavatories.

Penny Lane itself in 1936 – a sleepy side road.

Mosspits Lane School teachers on visit to Bruges, 1954. L–R: Miss Gabriel, unidentified, Miss Wainwright, Mr Roddy, Mr Barber.

Mosspits Lane School pupils on their visit to Bruges, 1954.

Aigburth Vale High School for Girls main building.

Aigburth Vale High School – sixth formers relaxing in a classroom.

Aigburth Vale High School staff, circa 1955.

With my cousin Jean on a trip to the Lake District with Auntie Dilys. We are proudly wearing school blazers.

My schoolfriend Irene Brightmer in school blazer with candyfloss.

Dale Street in 1946. The Municipal Buildings, centre, with clock.

Lewis's department store frontage – the statue popularly named Dicki Lewis greatly shocked my Auntie Nellie.

The Pierhead looking south, 1956.

The Pierhead, June 1949, with ferry boats.

Liverpool's last tramcar at The Pierhead,
September 1957. The Anglican cathedral is
in the background.

The last tramcar – Liverpool
Corporation's commemorative ashtray
– no fear of tobacco in 1957.

Statues of Bessie Braddock and Sir Ken Dodd at Lime Street Station.

Statues at the entrance to the Walker Art Gallery, 1945.

The Lord Mayor's coach, December 1947.

Holy Trinity Church before the demolition of its tower.

Interior of Holy Trinity, Wavertree.

Holy Trinity choir and clergy. My father, at left, holding people's warden's wand of office. Canon Taylor, who taught me Greek, seated next to the then Rector, Revd John Morris, centre.

My parents in the hall at 30 Heathfield Road.

Presenting a bouquet.

With Doreen (left) and June (centre) Wood in the backyard.

Calderstones Park Lake.

Cromwell.

Frisky Silky Bobbety Bun in the backyard at Heathfield Road.

With Kim, a Lakeland terrier, and my mother in the hall at 30 Heathfield Road.

With Kim and my friend Mary Delgarno in the backyard.

On holiday at Min-y-Clwyd, Ruthin, 1948.

Liverpool Show Silver Jubilee plate.

The Lord Mayor's carriage at the Liverpool Show in the 1950s.

Liverpool Show – The Police Procession, 1959.

Nanna and Ganger Butcher with their daughters.

At Chester Zoo with my mother and Belgian cousin.

My mother in Calderstones Park with Christine Batuwade.

My friends Janet McCormac and Mary Delgarno among Calderstones Park's flower beds.

My parents at Hale on the banks of the Mersey with my schoolfriend Anne Griffiths.

Robin's christening photograph. It enabled us to be reunited with him years later.

It was not surprising that my parents, with their experience of running the Life Boys in Norris Green, felt they should help Miss Davidson in her work with the poor boys of Wavertree. What was perhaps surprising was the fact that some of the staff working in the Town Clerk's Department gave money from their own pockets in a regular collection to help fund her care work.

Soon the boys living at The Little House became my friends. At first I found it difficult to imagine any mother handing over her son and his ration book to a stranger. Then, slowly, the boys talked to me about the neglect they had suffered. One boy described how he used to be left outside in his house's yard, tied with a rope to a bin, while his mother went out. If he soiled himself while she was away, she would whip him on her return.

The boys Miss Davidson took in were still at junior school and could not be relied on to attend church on their own. She took the Roman Catholic boys to her church, but the Church of England boys posed a problem. My parents solved that problem for her. They started taking the Anglican boys to their church, Holy Trinity, Wavertree. We must have looked a motley lot sitting in the pew: my father in his dark pinstripe suit and tie, my mother and me attired in clothes from posh stores, plus two or three Little House boys in their cast-offs.

Miss Davidson's insistence on the boys she took in being baptised prompted her to ask my parents to become godparents to any unbaptised potential Little House boy whose parents were Anglicans; they agreed to take on this responsibility. Holy Trinity church was to be the place for the baptismal ceremonies. As was usual in those days, the baptisms were subdued events. They were held in a small baptistry at the rear of the church and not during a general service.

One day, when my parents and I called at The Little House to give Miss Davidson some money, we were followed indoors by a policeman. He was calling to ask about a stolen bike. He strongly suspected it had been taken by one of the boys.

Police visits to The Little House were quite common and people usually took them in their stride. But this time the policeman's entrance created an unexpected uproar. Before the policeman said a word, my parents' latest godson ran towards Miss Davidson crying: 'I didn't do it. I didn't do it.' Alas, it transpired he had done it. The boy was crying because he thought the police knew he had set fire to Edge Hill railway goods depot, causing a quarter of a million pounds worth of damage. The godson disappeared from our lives that day, never to be heard of again.

Other boys stayed longer. My greatest friend was George. He stayed at The Little House for a few years and was just a couple of years older than me. One day, he gave me what was then his dearest and almost only possession – his bag of glass marbles. Such generosity was amazing and I treasure them to this day. The dirty cotton drawstring bag that held them has long gone, but I have added to George's collection over the years. Glistening on a large glass plate with lit candles standing among them, the glass marbles make me wonder what happened to my friend. Did he go straight, or did he end up in prison?

I have good reason to think George may not have gone straight. Although he was a kind person, his morality was a morality acquired among the deprivation of Liverpool's slums. For example, he explained to me that it was very wrong to rob the baker's shop in Wavertree High Street, because the baker worked for himself and lived among us. However, he also explained that it was quite in order to rob the Abbey Cinema up the road by the Picton Clock, because that was a big business owned by people from far away. The owners probably did not care much about that particular cinema, and anyway they had lots of money to spare.

After church the boys and I would often walk back to The Little House together, while my parents talked to their friends. At first my mother had severe doubts about entrusting her little pigtailed daughter to the ruffians, but my father persuaded her

I would be safe. Sometimes I was even allowed to go with the boys by bus to play in Childwall Woods.

During matins on Mothering Sundays, the children of Holy Trinity church were told to leave their pews and walk up towards the church sanctuary. There the rector would present each child with a small posy of flowers for them to give to their mother. Invariably the posies contained a mix of violets and primroses, surrounded by a few primrose leaves, and firmly tied with a piece of very thin white cotton. One year, as I handed my bunch to my mother, I wondered what the boys would do with their posies.

After the service, the boys and I said goodbye to my parents and headed off down the churchyard on our way to The Little House. It was a sunny day and the boys were still clutching their flowers. We had gone a short way through the graves when Michael stopped us. His bunch of flowers had put him in difficulties. He still sometimes saw his mother and he loved her, but he was staying with Miss Davidson and he loved her too. Like George and the other boys, he wanted to give Miss Davidson some flowers on Mothering Sunday, but he also wanted to give some flowers to his mother.

Together we considered Michael's problem. Then we solved it by pausing at a high, flat grave that looked a bit like a table. Michael placed the small bunch of flowers on the gravestone and untied the thin string. We watched as he divided the flowers and their leaves equally into two even smaller bunches: one violet for his mother, one violet for Miss Davidson, one primrose for his mother, then one primrose for Miss Davidson, and so on.

Miss Davidson's active membership of the Roman Catholic Church meant there were often visitors at The Little House. On one occasion my parents called there unannounced and found a bevy of French nuns sitting round the bare dining table. Miss Davidson took one look at my father and said: 'I knew the Lord would provide.' He did. My father went round to the fish and chip shop and bought them all supper.

The visitor I liked most at The Little House was the priest who gave gym lessons in the backroom upstairs. Sometimes, when he was expected, I was allowed to turn up in my shorts and join in. Nowadays, sadly, the idea of a Roman Catholic priest giving private gym lessons to young boys would be met with cynicism on the part of many people.

But that priest acted from the goodness of his heart. He knew there was quite a lot of traffic on the High Street, so it was not really a safe place to play out. He also knew that, if the boys roamed elsewhere in the neighbourhood, they were likely to be tempted into crime. There was no television or radio in the house and the boys were not keen on reading, so the gym lessons gave the boys something to do and used up some of their energy.

A large black tomcat, called Radar, sometimes watched our gym lessons. Miss Davidson believed in reverence for life and would not even kill a fly. She claimed she had trained Radar not to kill rats, mice, birds or cockroaches. It is hard to believe that, in a Liverpool slum at that time with all the rats and mice, Radar did not sometimes have an extra meal outside; but he certainly did not dare to bring the remains into the house.

The interior of The Little House was very gloomy. The windows were small and the walls dark. At times, the stench of urine from the beds of the maternally rejected boys was almost unbearable. But Miss Davidson soldiered on, feeding, clothing and caring for the boys as best she could. Her only other occupations were prayer and embroidery. The boys were not interested in the embroidery, but I was fascinated.

One of her embroidery projects was a map of Welsh saints that she was creating for a church in Holywell, north Wales. The jewel colours of the pure silks, imported from France, gleamed even in the gloom of the slum house. I soon realised that Miss Davidson's work was much more refined than the woollen tapestry which my Belgian Auntie Yvonne had taught me. So many shades could be used to create light, shade, feeling and depth of colour that a silk embroidery picture could seem as expressive as a watercolour painting.

Miss Davidson saw that her sewing fascinated me. On a small piece of linen she drew a picture of a Kentish apple orchard in May, then gave me some real silks to start embroidering it. Most of the work, depicting a path, grass and an oast house, was done in single strand silk long and short stitches. The apple blossom was different; the stitch I was told to use was French knots. Each knot was made from three strands of silk.

Miss Davidson showed me how to vary the colours of the strands so the French knot blossoms facing the sun at the very tip of the tree branches were palest pink, while those on the side of the trees away from the sun were embroidered in darker pinks. At the heart of the trees, she even encouraged me to combine a single strand of deep purple colour with the darker pinks. It worked, the subtle combination of colours created a feeling of perspective and depth.

Fascinated as I was by silk embroidery, it was hard going. My work of art took ages to complete. I was nine when I started it and nearly thirty by the time it was finished. Yet the delight in good embroidery that Miss Davidson taught me has not left me. Years later, visiting the Elizabeth Hoare collection of church embroidery in the tower of Liverpool's Anglican cathedral, I gazed in awe at the daisies on a vestment and the roses on an altar front. How devotedly the embroiderers must have worked to create such detailed beauty.

Looking at the ecclesiastical works of art in Liverpool's Anglican cathedral, I wondered what had become of Miss Davidson's embroidered map of Welsh saints. I know what happened to Miss Davidson. The hard work and poverty became too much for her. After moving to London, she ended her days in an east London hospice, devotedly cared for by Roman Catholic nuns. My mother travelled to London regularly to visit her until she died. She told me they often talked about The Little House, and hoped their work in that Wavertree slum had brought some light and sense of self-worth into the boys' lives.

Good works

THE YOUNG GIRLS sat in silent rows on wooden benches facing a wide bay window. Each held a baby in her arms. In front of the girls, rows of baby baths stood on long, low tables. The girls were all what, in the 1950s, were described as 'unmarried mothers'. Soon, their babies would be taken away from them and adopted. Before that parting, however, the mothers were expected to bath and feed their babies for six whole weeks. There were supposed to be medical reasons for this requirement; but it seemed to me that it must feel like purgatory and was probably intended to be a punishment for the sin of having a baby outside marriage.

My mother had volunteered to help teach baby feeding and baby bathing to the mothers. One day during school holidays she was unable to get somebody to look after me; that was why I stood at the entrance to the big room sensing the young mothers' fears and misery. The girls, some little older than I was, were trying to cope not just with a new baby, but also with rejection by their families and the judgement of a society that regarded them as fallen women.

The girls were looking out of the bay window when a car swept up the drive. Silence descended on the room. It seemed as if even the babies stopped crying. Everybody knew the car had come to take a baby away from its mother for ever.

Hung on a wall in another part of the home I saw a text about God being able to see you even in secret places. The home's residents were not allowed to forget their sins. Laughter seemed to have been abolished at St Monica's Church of England home for mothers and babies. The building was one of the most miserable places in the city.

St Monica's appalled me. It seemed so unforgiving. The

girls staying there had become mothers at a time when the availability of birth control was much more limited than it is today, and the methods available often unreliable. Before the contraceptive pill became widely used, it could be hard to gain information about methods of birth control. Advice was often confined to married women, and women in Britain did not begin to have access to the pill until 1961.

Moreover, knowledge of what, in the 1950s, was then guardedly referred to as the 'Facts of Life' was not as widespread as it is today. For many Liverpool children knowledge of human biology was learnt by a process of osmosis, or by visits to the Walker Art Gallery, where nudes and their activities could be viewed without adult intervention.

It is difficult to explain to people today just how secretive many adults were about the facts of life sixty years ago. My mother's best friend, married just before the outbreak of the Second World War, confided after her husband's death that, during a forty-year marriage, her husband had never seen her naked. Each evening she would change into her nightdress in the bathroom before retiring to bed. The bedroom light was kept firmly switched off, always.

Her friend's admission surprised my mother who was a bit more open on such matters. Nevertheless, after the headmistress of what was to be my new grammar school told parents they should tell their daughters the facts of life, she was quite put out. How could a respectable woman possibly discuss such matters with an eleven year old? She solved the problem that very afternoon. Walking along Allerton Road returning home from the school open day, she announced: 'The headmistress says we've to tell you the facts of life. Sex is like Holy Communion – a mystery.' She then added: 'Nanna Butcher always said your bedroom door has a lock on it for a reason.' And that was that.

Many of the girls at St Monica's had become pregnant as a result of ignorance rather than conscious irresponsibility. They had had a baby thanks to men, but the men were nowhere to be seen. In the 1950s men all too often escaped blame for an unmarried conception. There was a widespread feeling that the men were just doing what came naturally. Yet the pregnant unmarried women were labelled as brazen hussies who had brought shame upon themselves and on their parents. Rejected by their families, unmarried expectant mothers turned to places like St Monica's and the adoption services such places provided, because they simply had nowhere else to go.

At the time I could not understand why my mother would volunteer to help in such a place. Years later my mother became slightly more open about her feelings. I began to understand that, in doing good works like volunteering at St Monica's, she was trying to use her talents independently of men; but I never really understood how strong her motivation was until after she died.

Aged eleven, in 1925, my mother passed the scholarship examination to go to grammar school. This was very unusual at that time since there were few grammar school places for girls in the city. She felt proud and excited at passing the examination, but then her father refused to let her take up her scholarship. He did not, he said, believe girls should be educated to that level. As a consolation he bought her a collection of brown bound classic novels published by Odhams Press.

The novels were not enough compensation for the forced rejection of her scholarship. My mother adored her father, but all her life resented the way he deprived her of a grammar school education and a professional career. She was absent from secondary school for two years, developing a psychosomatic heart illness that made her unable to walk any distance.

Later my mother came up against more behaviour that, today, seems incredible and would be described as discrimination. Having worked in the accounts departments of Woolworths and Cooper's, the high-class grocery shop in Church Street, she was told that if she married she would have to give up work. This was a common thing to happen before the outbreak of the Second World War.

My mother wanted to get married so she did give up work; but she always resented the lack of opportunities to develop her talents independently. Much of her energy went into supporting my father's career development: in his legal studies to become a solicitor, and then in his rise from office boy to the top job of Town Clerk of Liverpool.

A naturally shy woman, my mother networked enthusiastically at city social events for her husband's sake; but she would rather have had her own career. When my father was awarded a British knighthood and became Sir Stanley Holmes, rather than Mr Holmes, my mother was delighted, particularly when he told her he could not have done so well without her support. She told me: 'It's for me as well', and revelled in the status she acquired from being called 'Lady Holmes'.

My mother's title could be embarrassing when, as she grew frailer, she was admitted to various hospitals. Like many elderly people of her generation who want to be called Mrs X or Miss Y when in hospital, she objected to young nurses and carers calling her by her first name. Feeling vulnerable in a hospital bed, she felt the staff who called her 'Doris' were being overfamiliar and demeaning her.

On each of her increasingly frequent hospital admissions, I would have to ask staff to replace the words 'Doris Holmes' on the label above her bed with 'Lady Holmes'. Some staff then just called her Lady, assuming that was her first name. One even commented to me that she thought Lady an odd name to call somebody, particularly as it was a dog's name in the film *Lady and the Tramp*.

My mother's good works were a substitute for the career she wished she had had. Many other women of my mother's generation were similarly treated by their fathers. Some of these women, particularly those who had not had large families to occupy their time, on seeing their daughters combining marriage, motherhood and career, became jealous and resentful of their own children. This made the waste of their talent and their lost opportunities even sadder.

Some of my mother's attempts to find good works to perform scarcely entered my consciousness because I was at school all day. I do recall her returning home in a nervous state after visiting a member of the church choir who was suffering from a mental illness and was confined in a men's locked ward in Rainhill Mental Hospital. One visit to Rainhill was quite enough for her. She had been terrified by the ravings of some of the patients and by the locking of the ward doors behind her.

Memorable too was the time my mother got involved with encouraging women who suffered from venereal disease to go on the straight and narrow. I never met any of the women. To protect me they were invariably invited to our house while I was out, but I usually knew when they had visited. After they left, my grandmother spent a long time on her knees scrubbing the bathroom lavatory remorselessly. She was worried that the lavatory's regular users would catch something from the seat.

After I had left Liverpool for university, my mother found great pleasure in her work with Salisbury House, the former Liverpool Orphanage. The orphanage had moved from the centre of the city to a purpose-built, three-storey brick building in Childwall a few years before the Second World War. The building, which has since been demolished, was very impressive and its grounds were large.

During the war, orphans were evacuated from Liverpool because of the bombing, and children did not return to the building until 1953. The ground floor was transformed into a school where local children as well as orphans were taught. Initially, orphans continued to be taken in and lived on the top two floors. However, changing patterns of social care, including an increasing use of fostering, meant that demand for orphanage services began to decline.

By the 1980s the building, which fifty years before had been seen as new and exciting, was considered too big, too costly to maintain and unsuitable to be used only as a day school. It was decided that a new school should be built in the grounds instead. By 1987 my mother had become Lady President of the Trustees of Salisbury House and laid the foundation stone for that new school.

Among the orphanage's few valuable physical assets were two Victorian oil paintings. My mother took them to London to be auctioned for the benefit of the charity. One picture was of a very pretty and healthy young girl attired in a white lace dress. It sold for a good price. How very different that young girl's life experiences must have been from the lives of the orphanage's residents.

The contents of the orphanage's button box, which my mother kept, gave an insight into the orphan children's lives. In my own button box, I still have some of its drab grey buttons for boys' shorts, the dark navy buttons for girls' skirts, the innumerable shirt buttons, and the tiny leather boot buttons with metal shanks; items successive matrons must have hoarded over the years.

Another group of children with whom my mother became involved were those who lived in a Dr Barnardo's home in Alexandra Drive, Liverpool. My parents became interested in the children housed by Dr Barnardo's soon after we moved to Penny Lane. My father's motivation was somewhat different from my mother's. It stemmed from an awful feeling that 'there but for the grace of God' went he. This feeling was generated not just by a fear of orphanhood aggravated by his mother's early death, but also by awareness that, as a young boy, he could easily have been labelled a juvenile delinquent and taken into care.

Apparently, one sunny day in Anfield, early in the 1920s, my father and a friend were at a loose end. To fill the time they decided to amuse themselves by taking somebody's low wall apart brick by brick. They were busy with this demolition job and making fast progress when some sort of instinct caused my father to move away and take an interest in other things. This was fortunate as, almost immediately, round a corner came a policeman. In those days there would have been no mercy shown to the demolition gang. Punishment would have been severe. My father suspected they would have been fortunate to have remained at home with their parents.

The children who lived in Liverpool's only Dr Barnardo's home were in some ways lucky. The home at 16 Alexandra Drive was run by Miss Patman and Miss Twaddell. The girls and I called them Auntie Dora and Auntie Rita. The aunties really loved their charges. When they retired from Barnardo's, they bought a house in Boston Spa, Yorkshire, and took some of the Liverpool girls with them. Thus they gave them the nearest possible thing to a real home.

The Liverpool Barnardo's home was a large building with a big asphalt playground at the back. It was not run as a home for Liverpool children; children were sent to it from different places around the country. Some of the girls could not remember where they came from, but one of the girls with whom I became quite friendly told me she had lived in Dartford, Kent.

It was not clear to me how Dr Barnardo's selected children for a particular home. Another of the girls, Irene, told me she thought a factor was an assessment of each child's intelligence, made when they were first taken into care at a young age. She was convinced that Dr Barnardo's had assessed her early on and not expected her to pass the 11+ examination. If that was so, Irene defied their expectations. After she passed the exam, she worried about where, in that noisy Alexandra Drive home, she would find a place to do her homework.

My parents' contribution to the home's running, which lasted all the time Auntie Dora and Auntie Rita were in charge, was threefold. First, they became lifelong friends of the aunties, thus giving them support in a difficult job. Second, they visited the home regularly, taking me along with them, to organise games in the playground and sing-alongs around the piano in the dining room. Third, from time to time, they invited one of the girls to stay at our house during school holidays.

I quite enjoyed sharing a bedroom with the girls who were invited to stay. Sometimes I listened as they told me tales of their past, but mostly we just played and enjoyed the present. The girls seemed to prefer that. I vividly recall the Easter when one of the Barnardo's girls stayed with us. We were each given a huge chocolate Easter egg. We tried to eat them in one go, while standing on our heads in the bedroom with our legs against the wall. My mother was not amused by the smears of chocolate all over the sheets.

But my best memories of the Barnardo's home are of us all – the girls, the aunties, my mother and me – standing around the piano singing together, while my father played any tune requested and told us jokes. Unlike my mother, my father could not read music; instead he played the piano by ear. That was a wonder to us all. One of the girls had only to sing him a pop tune once and he could play it well enough for us to sing along with him.

We also sang traditional songs around the piano in Alexandra Drive. We particularly enjoyed the songs we sang with actions. These included 'My Bonnie Lies Over the Ocean', 'Hang on the Bell, Nellie', and 'Under the Spreading Chestnut Tree'. As the sound of our singing resounded in the high-ceilinged room, you could sense happiness bubbling inside us all. The children living in that Barnardo's home might have been mistreated or rejected in the past, but with Auntie Dora and Auntie Rita they had found a haven of security, love and laughter.

Young ladies

THE SIGHT OF my friend Mary and me, ambling around the Liverpool Show enjoying our pink candyflosses, appalled my mother. 'Remember who you are,' she said, as she ordered us to put the delicious pink sticky stuff in a bin. We thought we knew who we were. We were a couple of young girls out enjoying ourselves; but my mother expected us to behave like young ladies, and that was a very different thing. Young ladies did not eat in public while walking along. Eating in public was vulgar or, in Liverpool terminology, common.

Like many other aspirant middle-class mothers in the 1950s, my mother started early trying to train her daughter to become a young lady. Young ladies knew how to dance; that is how eventually they hooked a man to marry. My mother was thinking of events like the debutante balls, which were still held when I entered my teens. They were not abolished until 1958. Since competence in dancing was useful in finding a man, I was sent to dancing lessons. I soon grew to hate them.

The dancing project was a long-term one. It started early with tap and ballet. The aim was to lay a foundation that would later develop into a love of ballroom dancing. When we lived near Norris Green the project was quite successful. My mother was delighted to see me on stage downtown in Hanover Street at the Crane Hall, which today is much changed, and is called the Epstein Theatre in honour of the Beatles' manager, Brian Epstein.

I was dressed up in costumes made from dyed lint and cardboard. My mother had dyed the lint herself, my grandmother had sewn it, and my father had made me a red cardboard hat and red cardboard cuffs. Clothes rationing was still in force at the time (it did not end until 1949), and no other suitable materials were available.

The move to Penny Lane meant a change of dancing teachers. I was enrolled at the Vernon Johnson School of Dance, based above shops on Allerton Road. Founded in 1918 it is still going and describes itself as: 'one of the longest running dance schools in Liverpool.' Over sixty years ago, I was sent there to learn tap and ballet. To my mother's dismay, I found the lessons very boring.

One day when, for the umpteenth time, we were standing in the mirrored room, pawing the ground with our tap shoes and singing 'Horsey, horsey don't you stop,' I rebelled. To my mother's shame and my delight, it was suggested that it might be a good idea if I did not continue at the Vernon Johnson School of Dance. I had been expelled.

But my mother did not give up. If I could not do tap and ballet, I could still be encouraged to learn ballroom dancing. In my mid-teens, I found myself with two school friends going down town to attend dancing lessons in a building off Bold Street.

A man and woman tried to teach us. In my case they were unsuccessful. That was my fault, but the man's damaged leg was not ideal for conveying dance rhythms. Waltz time should go: ONE two three, ONE two three etc., with the emphasis always on the first of the three notes in the bar of music. Alas, our teacher's gammy leg meant he went: ONE two THREE, one TWO three. I soon left.

In those days middle-class families almost invariably ate meals together at a table. Mealtimes were a focus for many mothers' attempts to turn their daughters into young ladies. Aspirant young ladies should learn to use cutlery properly and to hold an intelligent conversation over dinner, though they must not speak with their mouths full.

The sight of an elbow resting on a dinner table was bound to prompt the single-word rebuke: ELBOWS! We knew what to do: take them off the table immediately. At family parties a coded warning would sound: FHB – Family Hold Back. This meant that, because after the war there were still shortages and food rationing, there might not be enough food to go around, so we should be polite and let our visitors eat the sandwiches and jellies first. That was what nice young ladies and young gentlemen did, and it would be shaming to run out of food.

At parties my father's elder sister, Auntie Fran, was particularly hot on elbows and FHB. Unfortunately her husband, a Welsh-speaking art teacher and a bit wild at times, could usually be relied upon to lower the tone by deciding to sing:

Catherine ate jam.
Catherine ate jelly.
Catherine went to bed with a pain in her …
　　　[pause and giggles from children]
Don't be mistaken.
Don't be misled.
Catherine went to bed with a pain in her head.

My father, seeing my cousin Catherine's embarrassment, would try to make amends by embarrassing me instead. He sang: 'Mr Holmes's baby's got a mole upon her nose' to the tune of 'John Brown's Body'. I knew I had a mole on the end of my nose and hated to hear it mentioned. Sometimes Auntie Fran had a lot to put up with at those parties.

It was obvious to my mother that a Scouse accent did not go well with being a young lady. A Scouse accent was common. I must, therefore, be taught to speak properly. One of the best ways of doing this, it was decided, was by learning tongue twisters. I would sit at table learning:

She sells seashells on the seashore.
The shells she sells are seashells I am sure.

and:

Are you copper bottoming them, my man?
No I am aluminiuming them, mum.

My Belgian Auntie Yvonne, who lived in the same road, joined in the fun. To get rid of any traces of that awful Scouse accent, I should learn tongue twisters in French – even though at that time I had not learnt French at school. I sat at her table reciting:

Combien côutent ces six-cents saucissons ci?
Si ces six-cents saucissons ci côutent six-cents,
Combien côutent ces six-cents saucissons la?

If I had been able to understand French at the time, I might have wondered why on earth anybody would want to buy six hundred sausages and why, since cents was presumably short for centimes, they were so cheap; but I did not understand so just carried on reciting.

Aged eleven, I discovered my new school shared my mother's view of Scouse accents as a liability. To try to rid us of them, in our first year at Aigburth Vale High School for Girls, we had weekly elocution lessons. We were told to bring a mirror into school and hold it in front of our mouths to watch ourselves enunciating. Our elocution teacher was also an enthusiast for tongue twisters. This time the favourite was:

Betty bought a bit of butter
But she said 'my butter's bitter'
So she bought some better butter
To make her bitter butter better.

It was not just by her voice that you could tell a young lady. There were other ladylike things we had to learn at grammar school. A whole house, next to the school and called 'Gorselands', was devoted to teaching us how to become marriageable young ladies and good housewives. The house contained classrooms and a pretend flat that we were expected to learn to clean.

I enjoyed learning to sew at Gorselands, even though the things we were expected to make, like a pair of long-legged knickers, a pyjama case and a very antiquated looking nightdress, would never be used. Enthused by our teacher Miss Marshall's lessons on how to use a sewing machine, I even saved up to buy one. Its purchase was accompanied by six free sewing lessons in the Singer sewing shop on Bold Street. I began to make my own clothes on the machine. Being able to sew your own clothes was a useful skill to have, particularly so soon after the abolition of clothes rationing and before large-scale imports of cheap clothes.

While I found sewing lessons interesting, the domestic science lessons on cookery and cleaning were torture. Before members of the class cooked anything, they had to draw a plan. On a piece of paper, girls were expected to mark out where each implement they planned to use would be placed: a ladle here on the right, a whisk over there on the left, the mixing bowl in the middle etc. When we cooked we had to make sure we put each implement back in place in accordance with that plan. It all took so long and seemed so divorced from reality, I hated it.

I began to realise I might be a feminist the day we were taught how to clean shoes during a domestic science lesson in Gorselands. It was demonstrated to us that not only must we polish the tops of shoes; we must also polish the underside between the sole and the heel. This was particularly important in the case of men's shoes. In the years to come, if we cleaned shoes properly, when men knelt down at the altar rail in church, people would see the polished undersides of our husbands' shoes. Then they would notice what good housewives we were, because we had carefully cleaned the parts of our husbands' shoes that were not normally on view. Even then, I felt husbands should clean their own shoes. It is a good thing I eventually married a man who did National

Service in the Army; personal responsibility for shoe cleaning is ingrained in such men.

Musical accomplishments were something else which would mark us out as young ladies. Like many girls of my generation, I started off my musical non-career by taking piano lessons. Week after week, I trudged to Miss Aitken's house in Earlsfield Road, my leather music case in my hand.

After entering her house, I walked past her print of the Walker Art Gallery's picture *Faithful unto Death* by the Victorian artist Edward Poynter. It showed a Roman centurion bravely facing death by staying at his post while lava flowed from Mount Vesuvius during its eruption in AD 79. Then I entered her front room to sit at an upright piano for half an hour. Night after night, at home, I faithfully practised scales and set pieces; but I knew in my heart I was not a good piano player, and Miss Aitken's efforts were wasted.

My parents found my poor piano playing ability hard to understand. My mother was a good pianist and read music easily. My father could not read music, but he could play any tune by ear. I inherited neither of their abilities but, despite my lack of any piano playing talent, I was expected to keep practising. Young ladies did not give up.

Miss Aitken encouraged her pupils' love of music by taking groups to the Philharmonic Hall to listen to chamber music concerts. We were lucky that she was willing to do this. With her we heard the Amadeus String Quartet and other well-known musicians of the time. However, those visits to the Philharmonic reinforced my awareness that I was not a natural musician.

Trying to develop any latent musical talent I might have, Miss Aitken eventually took me down town to play pieces written for two pianos. A choirboy from the Anglican cathedral played the other piano. He was good. I was not. The experiment was not a success.

Eventually, Miss Aitken told my mother a sad truth: her daughter might be a whizz at musical theory, but she could not sing to pitch. Without that skill, there was no way she would make progress and pass higher piano examinations. My mother was mortified, but even then she did not give up. She contacted a music teacher at the C F Mott Teacher Training College in Prescot. The teacher was aptly named Miss Nightingale. Her verdict was clear: 'There are some people, Mrs Holmes, who are tone deaf. Your daughter is not tone deaf. She is tone dumb. Nothing can be done.' Piano lessons were soon abandoned.

Liverpool secondary schools also sought to develop the musical talents of the city's youth. Members of the Philharmonic Orchestra would visit schools to give concerts. Girls at Aigburth Vale High School particularly appreciated the visits of the flautist Fritz Spiegl.

The April Fools' Day concerts that Fritz Spiegl started in the Philharmonic Hall and his 'Concerto for Motor Horn and Orchestra' were particularly enjoyable. His sense of humour and innovative use of instruments could make classical music seem attractive to us schoolgirls. This was quite an achievement as our preferred music venue was a padded booth in Brian Epstein's record shop NEMS in Great Charlotte Street.

In NEMS, we listened to records and pretended we could afford to buy them with our pocket money. Lonnie Donegan, Pat Boone, the Everly Brothers, Marty Wilde, Cliff Richard, and the Liverpool-born singer Billy Fury, whose statue now stands at Albert Dock, were among the singers we asked to sample.

Alas, I missed out on the Beatles. They were only just beginning to form and called themselves the Quarrymen after Quarry Bank Boys' School, the school John Lennon attended. One day, somebody suggested that girls from Aigburth Vale School should go along to hear the Quarrymen. I was among those girls whose reaction to this invitation was unfavourable. We had no intention of going along to hear a skiffle group comprising boys from Quarry Bank and the Liverpool Institute – or 'Inny Ninnies' as they were sometimes referred to.

Instead of listening to the future Beatles in person, I visited the future Beatles' manager's record shop. My mother would not have been pleased if she had discovered that my school friend, Elizabeth, and I combined regular visits to the orthodontist in Rodney Street with downtown trips to NEMS.

For months, Elizabeth and I managed to book our dental appointments on the same day, at the same time, and during afternoon school. We always tried to ensure our appointment times made it impractical to return to school that same day. After our dentistry, we therefore felt free to visit NEMS before going home. It was, in its way, a sophisticated form of truancy.

Aigburth Vale High School, intent on developing its young lady pupils' classical music skills, decided I should try to learn the violin. My Auntie Yvonne gave me her late husband's instrument, explaining that her Ernie had left it on top of a wardrobe when he went off to sea during the war. He was a ship's radio operator. After a torpedo hit his ship somewhere off Australia, he had stayed in post, radioing SOS until he drowned. Auntie Yvonne told me that even the captain had abandoned ship, but not her Ernie. Like Miss Aitken's Roman soldier, he had stayed faithfully at his post to the last.

Unlike the piano, I enjoyed the violin; but violin lessons did not last as long as my piano lessons. Our then dog Kim, a Lakeland terrier, took against it. Somehow, my screeching down-bows on the E string affected his ears. He howled and howled, then in desperation bit my knee hard. Some years later, my father quietly burnt his cousin's violin. He explained apologetically that it had been adversely affected by water from a burst pipe. I am not sure I believed him.

Church was fun

'WE WENT TO church three times every Sunday.' People my age often accompany this statement with a groan or grimace, implying that church attendance was torture. It may have been for them. It was not for me at Holy Trinity Parish Church, Wavertree.

I do not know why my parents chose to attend Holy Trinity Church and not St Barnabas Church, which was nearer to our house and overlooked the roundabout at Penny Lane. Their choice involved a short walk not just down Heathfield Road but also along Church Road from the roundabout. I suspect they may have been influenced in their choice of church by architecture. Perhaps, having met among the relative simplicity of the art deco St Christopher's, Norris Green, they were attracted by the grey plaster walls of Holy Trinity.

There were, of course, periods of intense boredom in church, particularly when sermons at matins and evensong rambled on for thirty-five minutes and more. But there was also lots of fun to be had from active church membership. After the war very little other entertainment was available in suburban Liverpool, so for a lot of people church or chapel was the centre of their social life.

It was not until the Coronation Day in 1953 that my grandmother, who was living with us, saw a television set. She only saw one then because the church arranged to have a small television placed high in the church hall, so parishioners could watch the ceremony. The church hall was full that day as hardly anybody in the parish had a television.

On Coronation Day my parents took me on a day trip to Lake Windermere instead of to the church hall. When we stopped in Preston en route to the Lake District, all the other passengers got off the coach. They had travelled from Liverpool to Preston just to watch television at the homes of their friends and relations.

We travelled to Windermere by coach because, like most people, we did not have a car. Some time after the Coronation my Auntie Yvonne bought a car; but for much of my childhood she was the only person I knew who owned one. The absence of cars meant almost everybody travelled by public transport, and so did not go very far from home. For those who did not work in the city centre, even going down town could seem an exciting event.

Church services did have their pleasures. The choir sang anthems beautifully. The organist played well enough to give a concert. The vocabulary of the hymns could be exciting. I may not have understood a phrase like 'Consubstantial, coeternal, while unending ages run' but it had zing and challenged the intellect.

The church building itself was a source of pleasure to me. It is large and the architecture is Georgian. John Betjeman described it as 'Liverpool's best Georgian church'. Its stunted bell tower, the result of dangerous structure demolition in 1953, makes me doubt that now.

The church has wide window ledges. My friends and I enjoyed decorating them with fruit and flowers for harvest festivals. To this day the smell of chrysanthemums conjures up for me images of harvest time and autumn light. I find it unsettling to see chrysanthemums sold year-round, and even being used to decorate churches at Easter. Chrysanthemums should be autumn flowers.

My childhood three-service Sunday schedule started with matins at 11am. After that we went home for lunch. Children returned at 3pm for Sunday school, which was often held in the church hall. Later, at 6.30pm, there was evensong. Sunday school taught us Christian morality as well as Bible stories. 'Love thy neighbour as thyself' and 'Do good to those that hate you' became part of our lives.

If we attended and got things right at Sunday school, we were awarded stickers with Biblical pictures on them. The stickers were much prized, as were items such as the small cardboard bookmarks with pictures and religious texts that we were sometimes awarded. Some of the bookmarks were supposed to smell of carnations or violets, and so were particularly valued. We knew they could be bought in the Medici shop downtown in Bold Street, but we were not tempted to spend our pocket money on them; such things had to be won.

The big prizes were presented each year at the Sunday school prize-giving, held in the church hall across the road from the main church. The prizes were always books bought from the downtown booksellers, Phillip, Son & Nephew, who had a delightfully labyrinthine and dusty shop in Whitechapel.

No excuses for non-attendance at Sunday school were allowed. If you did not attend Sunday school regularly, you did not get a prize. As there was not much else to do on Sundays and because our parents thought attendance a good idea, most Sunday school members attended pretty regularly.

Another motivation for attendance was the annual Sunday school picnic. Once a year, we set out by coach through the Mersey Tunnel for the Wirral. After the excitement of driving through the tunnel, we reached distant destinations like Bidston Hill, Thurstaston Common and Arrowe Park in Birkenhead. Today, these places do not seem far from Liverpool; but, at that time, visiting them from the city was a great adventure. After arriving we played games like hide-and-seek, and ate our sandwiches before returning exhausted to the church where our parents awaited us.

The eventual aim of Sunday school was to lead us to become confirmed members of the Church of England; that would mean we could take Holy Communion. My mother was particularly excited at the thought of my confirmation, and told me she had been confirmed in the 1920s by Liverpool's greatly loved Anglican Bishop Chavasse. Sadly, she did not live long enough to see the new Chavasse Park in Liverpool One named after the bishop's VC-winning son.

My mother was determined to record the occasion of my confirmation and booked Albert Marrion, the Penny Lane photographer whose studio was next to the Welsh chapel, to take a confirmation photograph of me attired in a white dress, a white woollen bolero, and a white veil. For years the picture had pride of place on her music cabinet. I thought it was awful, but I blame the subject and not the photographer who everybody around Penny Lane knew was very good.

Holy Trinity church is flanked by two schools. On one side is the Blue Coat and on the other the Liverpool Blind School. The children from the Blind School attended Holy Trinity Sunday school. A family friend, Connie Clague, was their teacher. Connie had been made blind by measles: an illness that, before vaccinations were available, was much feared. After I had been confirmed, aged fourteen, Connie asked me to help her for a few weeks with a new teaching programme the Sunday school superintendent was introducing.

The new scheme, called 'Crossbearers', involved writing answers to questions. If an answer was correct, a square-shaped coloured sticker was stuck on the child's card. There were a number of differently coloured crosses on each card. To complete each cross, a child had to win six coloured stickers by answering six questions correctly.

The aim of Crossbearers was to complete all the crosses and win a series of badges. This seemed complicated, but Connie was sure the blind children would enjoy it. They would be able to feel the stickers on their cards with their fingers. They could type out their answer in Braille each Sunday and she would mark them during the week. I agreed to help Connie for a short time while she and the children got used to things.

Unfortunately, after week one, Connie had to go into hospital. I was left, aged fourteen, in charge of a class of children scarcely younger than me. How was I to keep control?

For the accidental Sunday school teacher there was only one thing to do: lie.

As the children could not see what I looked like, I pretended to be in my twenties. I had to mark the children's Braille answers, using a translated alphabet on the back of a Braille *Radio Times*. Pencil in hand, I laboriously marked up the children's work letter by letter, raised dots by raised dots, so I could then read it and mark it.

The Blind School children were very well behaved, except when Mr Bruce, the Sunday school superintendent, started prayers. He would say: 'Hands together. Shut your eyes.' I soon learnt that was a point to keep my eyes open. The children, thinking I could not see them because I had obeyed the instruction to shut my eyes, took the opportunity to sidle up to each other and pinch each other – the bottom was the preferred pinch location.

The children's personal prayers could be heartbreaking. I could hardly control myself when one newly arrived, and newly blind, child told me he was praying for his sight back. Jesus, he explained, could heal the blind.

The children often told me how much they enjoyed being at the Blind School, particularly playing football with a ball that had a bell inside it. However, their future job prospects seemed bleak. Connie used to remark that, for people like her, there was then little on offer in the way of training or employment except piano tuning, telephony and basket making. She chose telephony and worked for a time with the Guide Dogs for the Blind organisation.

Holy Trinity's church hall was also the place in which the church drama group met. Their performances were great fun, and for many in the congregation the only time they went to the theatre. Children always had the best view of performances. We sat at the back of the hall on low chairs placed on top of wobbly trestle tables. Today's health and safety experts would have a fit at the sight of such an arrangement, but the risk of tumbling off the table by wriggling around and making it wobble was all part of the fun.

The most regular users of the church hall were the various youth organisations that met there. Younger boys attended Life Boys and older ones the Boys' Brigade in it. Holy Trinity's Brownie pack also met in the hall. Later on, when boys and girls reached fourteen, they could join the church youth club that was also held in the hall.

Brownies was fun. When we met we would start by forming a big circle and skipping round a papier mâché toadstool, singing: 'We're the Brownies, here's our aim. Lend a hand and play the game.' The Brownie pack was divided into named sixes. After that song, each six would break in turn from the main circle, join hands and dance round the toadstool singing their six song.

I was in the Welsh Tylwyth Teg six. Our song was:

Here we come, we're Tylwyth Teg.
Dance and work and never beg.

One of my friends was a Pixie; she was: 'Helping others when in fixes.' Another friend was a gnome; the gnomes were: 'Helping mothers in their homes.' The assumption of the gnome six's ditty was based on reality. Housework was almost always women's work, and it was seen as natural for children to expect their mothers to do all the work in the home.

Later in the evening, the Brownies played games. Creeping Bunny was considered particularly exciting and the silence accompanying it must have given Miss Hayes, our leader called Brown Owl, great pleasure.

To play Creeping Bunny we stayed seated cross-legged in our circle while one child knelt in its centre and, bent over with her eyes shut, tucked her hat into the back of her brown leather belt. The idea was that the other Brownies, each in turn, crept around the outside of the circle, then into the circle itself. There they had to snatch the hat from the belt, all without being heard. The child in the centre had to listen and point if she heard a noise. If she pointed at the child who was creeping around, that child was out. Then another child tried to get the hat. That may not sound very exciting to today's children, but we thought it fun at the time.

The Brownies' best feature was the badges. We sewed them on the sleeves of our brown dresses and competed to get as many as we could. Some of the things I learned then, like tying knots, have stayed with me and proved useful. Other skills remain but their usefulness has been lost. This is particularly true of the, then much valued, art of sock darning.

In the years just after the war sock darning was an important skill. It was part of the ability to make do and mend which was essential when so many goods were in short supply or rationed.

I loved darning and borrowed my grandmother's wooden toadstool to put under the holes so that my work was particularly neat. I still have that shiny wooden toadstool. It sits on top of a bookcase. Most people who notice it do not have a clue what it was used for. Nurtured on television antiques programmes, some visitors remark wisely: 'Ah. A piece of treen,' but I suspect that is as far as their knowledge goes.

Moving up to the 115th Liverpool Girl Guides was exciting, particularly as, to begin with, it met in a former barn off Hunters Lane. The barn was very ramshackle and set in a cobbled yard. It was a lone reminder of Wavertree village's agricultural past. Soon we were forced to leave it and meet instead in the hall of my former junior school – Mosspits Lane. One Sunday a month, with the other uniformed church youth groups, we went to church en masse and paraded our flag up to the altar at the start of the service.

Our Guide leader was Miss Parry. Each summer she took us camping. Her real love was Anglesey. We headed off to that island in the back of a large John Mason removal lorry. The bottom flap at the back of the van was closed up to ensure we did not fall out. The top flap was kept open so we could see out and get fresh air. Sitting on our army-style kit bags, we sang and sang. In the days before motorways and bypasses, it was a long way to Anglesey.

On arrival at a farm, bell tents were put up, latrines dug and a campfire lit. After cooking on the fire, we would sit around and sing. The gibberish 'Ging Gang Goolie' which was supposedly written by Baden-Powell, the founder of the Scout movement, and the Australian song 'Waltzing Matilda' were among our favourites. Another song we delighted in was the traditional sea shanty 'Donkey Riding'. We knew some alternative words to the tune, including 'Were you ever in Llanddulas, Where to sleep the scouts did lull us?' Such words did not go down well with Miss Parry, who also disapproved of the alternative words we knew to the tune of 'Coming 'Round the Mountain'.

If the weather was fine the next day, we would indulge in activities like map reading with a view to adding to our Guide badge collections. However, there always seemed to be a problem with Anglesey: rain and more rain. When a deluge started, Miss Parry did not panic. Instead she told us to make sure water could not get into our tents by keeping the groundsheets inside. She also warned us not to touch the canvas tent sides because, if its sides were touched, a tent would leak.

But as the rain continued and the water rose, the tents started leaking anyway and eventually Miss Parry gave an order to evacuate. We moved our possessions to a barn where we slept the night in our sleeping bags. Unfortunately, we still had to make very wet and miserable journeys to the latrines that we had dug at the far side of the camping field. The next day, the John Mason lorry arrived to take us back to Liverpool, our camping holiday again cut short.

One year, presumably fed up with the Anglesey rain, Miss Parry decided to take us camping in the grounds of Chirk castle on the Welsh border instead. The camp was fun, but short. Again we were washed out by rain. That time we spent the night before our traditional emergency return to Liverpool in the equally traditional John Mason removal lorry, sleeping on a squash court. It made a change from a barn.

As we got older one of my friends and I encountered a problem with Guides' meetings. They were held on the same evening as the church youth club. We discovered we could go to Guides taking our glad rags with us, change out of our Guide uniforms in Mosspits Lane School's lavatories and then go on to the youth club. Miss Parry noticed our sadly diminishing enthusiasm for Guiding activities. She was deeply disappointed in us. Eventually, she announced that she thought we were 'more interested in the boys at the youth club than in Guiding'. Thus it was that, with happy hearts, and to our parents' misgivings, we were effectively expelled from Guides.

We should have been more grateful to Miss Dorothy Parry. She devoted almost all her spare time to Guiding, took us to camps and church parades, and encouraged us, through the taking of Guide badges, to acquire knowledge and develop skills which are still useful well over half a century later.

Taking a badge about trees I discovered, thanks to my honorary Uncle Mac, who was then Deputy Director of Liverpool's parks and lived in Calderstones Park, that there was a tree in the park called a tulip tree. We now have a tulip tree struggling for life among the elms in our Pembrey garden. Taking a badge about music, I was tested by a distinguished local musician on my appreciation of classical music and the lives of composers. The little I can remember from that test can still be useful when listening to Classic FM on the radio.

My memory of taking the Guides' childcare badge is the one that has stayed with me most clearly. It epitomised aspects of the city that, fortunately, have long gone. I was fourteen and part of the childcare badge involved putting children to bed. Miss Parry had made arrangements for me to do this at a local authority children's home. There was no need to obtain a criminal record check as that procedure had not been invented, and people were usually assumed to be innocent until proved guilty.

It was a time when single parenthood was a great family disaster. Such was some mothers' shame and isolation that babies were quite often left on doorsteps by their distraught mothers. These foundlings were then taken to children's homes to be cared for.

Sometimes, a mother left a note with her abandoned baby, but often nobody knew anything about a baby's background, including its religion. Liverpool City Council's policy on the religion of foundlings taken into its children's homes reflected the religious divide that then existed in the city. Foundlings of unknown religion were baptised alternately into the Roman Catholic and Anglican churches.

Soon after arriving at the children's home to take my Guide badge, I discovered that the children's awareness of difference between the two Christian sects was considerable, and far greater than mine. They lived in a city where, at the time, slogans of hatred were, as in Northern Ireland, painted on walls by each side of the Christian divide. 'Down with the Pope' was about the mildest of these.

When I started to put the children in the home to bed for my Guide badge, they said: 'We'll go, Miss, if you tell us. Are you Catholic or Protty Totty?' Stunned, I quoted the Apostles' Creed and told them I was both a Catholic and a Protty Totty, because I was a Protestant who believed in 'The Holy Catholic Church and the Communion of Saints.' That silenced them and I soon had them all tucked up in bed.

Thirty years later, by the time of my father's funeral at Holy Trinity church, where he had served as People's Warden for many years, the divide of hatred between Roman Catholic and Protestant had been greatly reduced. My father's great friend, the Anglican Bishop of Liverpool, David Sheppard, conducted the funeral in 1987. A Roman Catholic bishop also took part in the service. I noted the presence in the congregation of Jewish friends and a Welsh Presbyterian minister.

I found myself crying not just with sadness at my father's death, but also from a sense of deep relief for the city he had loved. The religious differences that had promoted so much hatred in my childhood were fading away. Trying to heal Liverpool's deep divisions between Roman Catholic and Protestant, Archbishop Worlock and Bishop Sheppard had frequently pointed out that the street, which runs between their two cathedrals, is called Hope Street. By their actions, they had brought hope to the city.

Murderering chess player – they said

THE JURY AT Liverpool Assizes in St George's Hall took just an hour to convict William Wallace of killing his wife Julia. He was condemned to death by hanging. Yet he said he loved her and had not murdered her. What is more, he thought he knew who had really killed Julia Wallace.

From his prison cell Mr Wallace sent a message to his friend, Mr Caird, asking if my father could go and see him in Walton Jail. My father, who was eighteen at the time, had known Mr and Mrs Wallace and Mr Wallace's friend, Mr Caird, since childhood. He became convinced Mr Wallace was not a murderer.

My father never got over his visit to the condemned man in his cell. When the abolition of capital punishment was being discussed, he argued strongly in favour of abolition. He supported his arguments by pointing out that an innocent person he knew had been on the point of being hanged for a murder he did not commit.

At Walton Jail, Mr Wallace told my father the name of the man he thought was the murderer. My father always believed that the man Mr Wallace named was in fact Julia Wallace's killer. That man was a few years older than my father, but my father had known him from the time when he was a pupil at Lister Drive School. He was clever, but he was also a bad lot. Some years after the murder, my father saw that man in a dock accused over a different matter for which he was convicted.

But when I asked my father to name the man Mr Wallace alleged was the murderer, my father's solicitor's training took over. He always refused to tell me. Instead, he would talk to me about the importance of people being considered innocent until proved guilty. It was most frustrating, particularly as my father had told my mother the name of the suspect. My mother said she had also known the young man in question when she was a teenager. She said he was a bit older than her. She also felt he could have murdered Julia Wallace, and said people in the neighbourhood thought he was a bad lot.

Mr Wallace was an insurance agent and a chess player. On Monday, 19 January 1931, the night before his wife was murdered, he went down town to the Central Chess Club, which met in the City Café in North John Street. He was scheduled to play in the Second Class Championship. As is normal in chess clubs, the arrangements for the match had been displayed on a noticeboard at the café well beforehand.

About half an hour before Mr Wallace arrived at the café, Samuel Beattie, the club captain, took a phone message from a Mr Qualtrough asking Mr Wallace to call on him the next night, Tuesday, 20 January 1931, at 7.30pm.

To many people, Qualtrough seems an odd name; but it is a Manx name and in those days the Liverpool Manx Society was very active. Mr Qualtrough gave his address as 25 Menlove Gardens East. Samuel Beattie conveyed the message to Mr Wallace. On the night before the murder, assorted members of the club, including Mr Wallace's good friend Mr Caird, discussed how to get to Menlove Gardens East.

Telephones in private homes were rare in the 1930s. If they wanted to make a phone call most people went to phone boxes standing in the streets. There they fed the apparatus by putting pennies in a slot, then asked an operator for a number. After the operator tried the wanted number, the caller pressed one of two buttons. If they pressed button A, they got through to the number. If they pressed button B, they got their pennies back. Sometimes, to the delight of local children, people pressed button B but forgot to collect their pennies; that is why, on the way to Mosspits Lane School, my friends and I would sometimes pop into the phone box on Heathfield Road to see if we could add to our pocket money.

That evening the phone message for Mr Wallace was made from a box a few hundred yards from Mr Wallace's home. It was memorable to the operator and to Samuel Beattie, partly because the person who made it pressed the wrong button the first time an operator spoke to him, and so had to speak to the operator a second time.

The next night, Tuesday, Mr Wallace left his house at 29 Wolverton Street, Anfield, and set off to visit Mr Qualtrough in the hope of getting new insurance business. The Menlove Gardens area runs off Menlove Avenue on the south side of the city and is quite a distance from Anfield.

Mr Wallace took two trams to get to his 7.30pm appointment. On the tram conductor's advice, he changed trams at Penny Lane roundabout. He did not know exactly where Menlove Gardens East was, but he knew the general Menlove location.

When he got to the Menlove area, Mr Wallace wandered around for some time. He asked a number of people, including a policeman, for directions; but he could not find Menlove Gardens East.

I have some sympathy with his predicament. If he had been seeking Menlove Gardens West, North or South he would have found them; but Menlove Gardens East does not exist. My parents, in their old age, moved nearby to 44 Green Lane. Neither they nor I could ever remember which was the one compass point absent among the Menlove Gardens, but we always knew there was a compass point missing.

Being unable to find Mr Qualtrough's house, Mr Wallace headed for home. When he got to Wolverton Street, about 8.45pm, he could not at first open the doors and was concerned. He did not believe his wife would have gone out since she had a cold. A next-door neighbour saw him in the back entry and urged him to retry the back door. This time it opened and Mr Wallace went inside.

At first he went upstairs, thinking his wife would be in bed.

Then, in the front room downstairs, Mr Wallace found her lying on the floor in front of the gas fire. Her body seemed cold and she had been bludgeoned to death. So violent had been the attack that the room walls were splattered with blood. Under the victim's head was a mac belonging to Mr Wallace. The mac, which was normally kept in the hallway, was soaked with blood. When the police looked at it they discovered singe marks, as if somebody had tried to burn the mac, then changed their mind.

Mr Wallace worked for the Prudential Insurance Company and kept money he collected in a box on the mantelpiece in the front room. He paid a week's takings in on Wednesdays. This meant that normally there would have been quite a bit in the box on a Tuesday night, but Mr Wallace had not had a good week. He was not a well man and that week had been quite ill, so had not collected all the money he should have. He had also had to make quite a few payouts. He thought only about £4 had gone from the cashbox.

Two days after the murder Mr Wallace told the police the name of the person he thought had murdered his wife. That young man gave them an alibi – his girlfriend. The police do not seem to have checked this alibi. The medical examination of Julia's body was perfunctory. Four days after the murder the police began to say they suspected Mr Wallace had murdered his wife. On 2 February 1931, thirteen days after his wife's murder, Mr Wallace was arrested, and by 25 April 1931 he had been sentenced to death.

The police theory was that Mr Wallace had himself made the Monday phone call to the Central Chess Club. If he had done so, it is odd that Mr Beattie did not recognise his voice. On the day of the murder Mr Wallace was alleged by the police to have stripped naked, put on the mac found under Julia Wallace's head, and bludgeoned her to death. His frequent attempts to find Menlove Gardens East that evening were put down to his desire to be noticed and so establish an alibi.

Problems like the complete absence of blood on Mr Wallace's

body or on the clothes he was wearing, and the absence of a murder weapon were ignored. The problem of timing was also largely glossed over. On the night of the murder, witnesses had seen Mr Wallace on the 7.06pm tram from Lodge Lane to Penny Lane. The stop where he got on the tram was quite a distance from 29 Wolverton Street, and Mr Wallace was a sick man. It would have taken him some time to walk to the tram stop from his house.

The last person to see Mrs Wallace alive was a local boy who delivered milk. Immediately after the murder, he told three people he had seen Mrs Wallace on her doorstep at 6.45pm. This would definitely have been after Mr Wallace left for the tram stop; but by the time of the trial, the boy was saying he saw her about 6.30pm. Even if that time was correct, it is hard to visualise even a fit man stripping off, putting on the mac, bludgeoning a woman to death, cleaning himself up completely, putting on his clothes, disposing of the murder weapon and walking to the tram stop in such a short time.

Mr Wallace appealed against his conviction and won the appeal on the grounds that there was no evidence against him. Sadly, he never recovered from the tragedy. He left Anfield, crossed the River Mersey and went to live on the Wirral. To his friend Mr Caird's great sadness, he died two years later, on 26 February 1933.

Julia Wallace's murder, her husband's conviction and appeal echoed through my childhood. My father had been deeply affected by his visit to Walton Jail. He knew the people involved, including the person Wallace believed had murdered his wife. He also knew Mr Wallace's great friend, Mr Caird. Mr Caird owned a grocer's shop in Anfield, and my father was friendly with his two sons.

As a child I used to accompany my parents to visit Mr Caird. The visits were enjoyable, particularly so because the Cairds were early owners of a television set. Like many of my generation, I did not have a television at home until I was in my mid-teens, so I was fascinated by this new invention.

While my parents and the Cairds talked and drank tea, I would sometimes be allowed to watch the grainy black-and-white pictures on the television in their front room.

However, most of the time the wooden cabinet doors, that hid the television screen from sight when the set was not in use, were shut. Sometimes on our visits my father or I played chess with Mr Caird. He would often sigh at the start of a game, remarking sadly that he used to play chess with his friend Mr Wallace on the very set we were using.

In an upstairs room at the Cairds' house was a collection of chess books. On some visits I was allowed to look at these while the grown-ups talked downstairs. Mr Caird explained that he and Mr Wallace had had a system for collecting chess books. One or other of them would buy one, but not read it. They would then play a series of twenty-four games. Whoever won the most games would be allowed to keep the book.

Mr Caird was said by my father to be a better player than Mr Wallace, and this might have explained the size of his book collection. In conversation Mr Caird always referred to his friend as 'Mr Wallace'. He never mentioned Mr Wallace's first name. I suspect it was a way of showing his respect for a much-demeaned man.

I enjoyed playing chess. Indeed it is my proud boast that I once came third in the British Girls' Chess Championship. This achievement is somewhat devalued by the fact that only four girls went in for it. As another Liverpool chess player, the Merseyside MP Angela Eagle, who won the British Girls' Championship in 1978, has pointed out, chess was then very much seen as a man's game and sexism was rife. Even today among the chess-playing fraternity, women's play is widely deemed naturally inferior to men's.

In the 1950s there was no gender separation in the huge chess congress that a local teacher, Mr Beech, organised each Easter holiday at the Liverpool Collegiate School. Girls competed in the same sections as boys, and hundreds of children attended. However, at the closing ceremony, if a girl won a prize a ripple of surprise spread through the hall. On one occasion when I went up on the platform to receive a prize, I heard the presenter exclaim in shock: 'It's a girl.'

To enable so many children to play the game, chess sets were brought into the Collegiate School from all over the city. The oldest and best child players would compete in a tournament that was held in the school library. These children had the honour of playing with the beautiful, heavily weighted Staunton Chess Sets belonging to Liverpool Chess Club. Children would tell each other: 'Wallace, the murderer, played with these pieces.' It was probably true that Wallace played with them because by the 1950s Liverpool Central Chess Club was no more, and the main chess club in the city was the Liverpool Chess Club. However, it now seems certain he was not a murderer.

When I first joined it, the Liverpool Chess Club met in Sampson & Barlow's Café in London Road. The popular Liverpool folk group The Spinners also held events there. Soon The Spinners became so popular that the chess club was evicted and found new premises in a gloomy building near Exchange Station. I had a feeling that the reason for the eviction was that The Spinners' fans spent more money than the chess players who were a quiet lot and made each drink last as long as possible. It is not conducive to winning a game to be drunk in charge of a chessboard.

Like me, my son became a chess player, but when I asked him if he hoped his own son would play chess he said: 'No!' He had had great fun playing the game, but he hoped his son would play rugby instead. I had great fun playing chess too, but I understood how he felt. Chess players, with their powers of concentration and need for forward thinking, can seem odd to non-players and even to fellow players. Think of the late Bobby Fischer, the famous world chess champion.

Mr Caird and my father believed that the nature and image of chess players had been part of Mr Wallace's problem with the jury. He was a tall, cadaverous-looking man. His gangling form looked odd and he was suffering from a kidney illness, so his skin was sallow. These looks, combined with his interest in chess, had counted against him at the trial. Mr Caird and my father thought jury members might have had an image of chess players as odd individuals capable of thinking well ahead about complex problems; consequently the jury may have reasoned that, as the case put forward by the prosecution about Julia Wallace's murder was so complex and involved considerable advance planning, only a chess player could have done it.

Many people have written about the Wallace case, but the book by Roger Wilkes – *Wallace: The Final Verdict Who Really Murdered Julia Wallace?* – fascinates me. In that book Roger Wilkes names the man Mr Wallace told both the police and my father he suspected had killed Julia Wallace. It is the bad lot who had helped out Mr Wallace on his insurance rounds a few times. He knew where Mr Wallace kept his insurance money, and had visited the Menlove area of the city. Julia Wallace would have let him into the house because she knew him.

Roger Wilkes's book also suggests an answer to a question that only came to my mind after my parents' deaths: why would Mr Wallace have asked my father to go and see him in his cell after his conviction? I had always assumed it was because he knew my father was studying law. But my father was born in December 1912. At the time of the murder, in January 1931, he was not even nineteen years old, so he could not have known much law by then.

I learnt from Roger Wilkes's book that an uncle of the man named by Mr Wallace as the murderer was the Liverpool City Librarian at the time of the murder. Moreover, the father of the alleged murderer worked in the City Treasurer's Department and, when he retired in 1950, had travelled up through the ranks of the city's administration to become Assistant City Treasurer.

In those days Liverpool's local government bureaucracy was nowhere near as large as it is today. Staff from different departments met together socially and there was a great deal of networking between them after, as well as during, office hours. At times children were also involved in the networking, and friendships lasting even to the present were formed; among them mine with Geoff Swinney, who painted the picture on the cover of this book.

The adult networking took many forms. My father loved reminiscing about a Town Clerk's Department's annual dinner for which he had booked a very amusing young man to provide the entertainment. The amateur comedian was brilliant and became a full-time entertainer the next day: his name was Ken Dodd.

Each year my father and a group of friends, including other Corporation officials, sometimes went by coach on a boys' jaunt to places like Blackpool. An annual cricket match between the Town Clerk's Department and the City Treasurer's Department was held at Sefton Park Cricket Club. Children of Corporation officials sometimes benefited from the inter-departmental network. A particular highlight for me was a visit to Mr Jones's house – Jones Roads – he showed us cartoons and silent Charlie Chaplin films on his home cinema equipment.

The Liverpool City Police, who investigated Julia Wallace's murder, only covered the city itself, and at the time of Mrs Wallace's murder were very much part of the city's local government network. Officials from the Town Clerk's Department regularly attended police displays. One year, at the Liverpool Police Horse Show, I sat next to my parents on a chair with a folded mac lying on it. I thought the mac would act as a cushion and give me a bit more height. It was unfortunate that the Chief Constable's hat was hidden under the mac. It got a bit squashed.

Mr Wallace would have been well aware of the close relationships that then existed between the various parts of the city's administration. He knew that my father worked in the Town Clerk's Department, and so would be likely to know some of the City Treasurer's Department's staff and might know some of the police.

Could it have been that, in his terrible situation, Mr Wallace asked to see my father because he suspected the city's local government establishment wanted to protect the son and nephew of one of their own, and that the case against him was brought to do just that? Might he have hoped that my father would understand that a close relationship between the officials of the various council departments could lead to a miscarriage of justice?

I will never know the answer to those questions. Even if I had been able to ask him when he was alive, I suspect my father would not have commented on Mr Wallace's motives for asking to see him. However, I now believe that the man Roger Wilkes said murdered Julia Wallace was the young man my parents knew and thought was a bad lot – and very possibly a murderer.

In hospital

THE GIRLS WERE discussing how long they had to live. One expected to last until she was fourteen, another to eight years old. Not all of us, patients in that general medical ward of Alder Hey Children's Hospital, had found out when we were expected to die, but some had. We children all found it an interesting topic of conversation.

The children who knew they did not have long left were amazingly philosophical about the shortness of their lives. They knew they were sick; that was why they were in hospital. They also knew some illnesses were incurable; there was, after all, a hospital near Liverpool city centre called The Home for Incurables. The Home was one of the caring institutions the nineteenth-century social reformer Josephine Butler had initiated in the city. She was the wife of the headmaster of Liverpool College, a boys' school that was private until September 2013 when it became an academy.

Those children who knew how long they were expected to live had discovered their prognosis thanks to the way Liverpool medical students were taught in the mid-1950s. When students were expected on a ward, a blackboard was placed by a child's bed. After a pause, in trooped the students and their lecturer.

It was thought unnecessary to put curtains round the bed, so the other children watched fascinated as the students examined the patient. After the physical examination, the patient was sent out to play on the ward's balcony. A lecture, complete with diagrams and words chalked on the blackboard, was then given round an empty bed. From their beds the remaining girls, who had not been sent out to the balcony, listened to that lecture with interest.

After the students, lecturer and blackboard had departed,

the sick child was allowed to return to her bed. Her fellow patients then repeated to her a rather garbled version of the lecture about the illness she was suffering from. This sometimes included how many years it was thought she had left to live.

Unlike the poor children with cystic fibrosis, or those suffering after-effects of rheumatic fever or polio, I was fortunate. I was not dying or severely disabled. I just had a tapeworm lodged far too firmly in my intestine. The day I discovered some of its extreme length exiting my body, and tried to pull it out but felt its suckers gripping my innards, was terrifying. Worse in a way was my immediate admission to Alder Hey Hospital.

That night, in 1955, my parents left me in the hands of an NHS which, when treating an illness, often lost sight of the feelings and fears of children suffering that illness.

Desperately in need of reassurance, I was informed by hospital staff that I would not see my parents again for days because visiting was confined to two days a week – Sundays and Wednesdays. As there was no bed available in a medical ward, I spent one night in a broken-leg ward. All was gloom there. The only light came from a table near the ward entrance where a nurse sat, head bowed, yet seemingly awake.

Up and down the long, shadowy ward, children lay on baize green covered beds. Their broken legs were set in plaster and held up in the air by weighted pulleys. Some whimpered. Some cried out loudly for their mothers. Each time I woke, the nurse was sitting by her lamp, seemingly unmoved by the children's cries of pain, looking down at whatever was on her table.

It was a relief next day to move to another ward and start treatment. The worm and I were starved. For three days only water passed my lips. By the third day, I had almost convinced myself I was not hungry. Unfortunately that day, an orderly, supervising the ward tea for ambulatory patients, had a problem. She sat down on a small chair at the end of a low table in the centre of the ward. The children, seated in two rows on either side of her, were about to eat when the orderly counted heads.

Suddenly the orderly looked horrified. There were thirteen at the table. Thirteen at the table was considered unlucky. There had been thirteen at the Last Supper, and look what happened then. Another child must be found to make the number up to fourteen. I was that child. 'I'm not allowed to eat,' I protested, but in vain. Sipping water, I was forced to watch my fellow patients munch their sandwiches and cakes. I felt hungry after all.

One day, the ward occupants became agog on my behalf. We were told I was to have an important visitor who was a man. When a visitor was expected on the ward all the patients were put to bed. So there we all were, in bed under the pristine sheets, waiting in silent expectation for my important male visitor. Apart from doctors, who all seemed to be men, we were not used to seeing men on that girls' ward. The nurses and orderlies were all women. Who then was this important man? What would he say?

The man arrived, flanked on each side by a nurse. The trio walked up the ward towards my bed. All the children's eyes were on them. The party halted three feet away from the end of my bed. The nurses looked up at the important visitor and waited for him to speak. The patients also waited in silent expectation.

'Harrumph. Wrong Ann Holmes,' announced the important visitor disgustedly. Agitated, the nurse on his right said: 'There's another one in the ward opposite.' Without a word of greeting or farewell, the trio departed. We all felt terribly let down. I was left wondering what the other child with the same name as mine was like, and if she was very ill.

At last, the day of my release came. The medical view was that all that was needed, before I was allowed to go home and after three days of starvation, was a giant dose of a yellow liquid called Mepacrine. This foul-tasting stuff was so awful and toxic that it would stun the worm. Its suckers would stop sucking and like magic it would fall out of my body. 'It worked with soldiers during the war,' I was told. 'It will work with you.' Alas it did not work with me. The hospital sent us both home.

Return to Alder Hey was inevitable, but I managed to put it off for two years. By 1957, nursing attitudes were slightly less rigid. The nurses seemed more aware of their patients being children, as well as of the children's illnesses. We were not confined to our beds as much and were allowed to play on the ward balcony more often. An attempt was made to give us very basic schoolwork. Symptomatic of the more relaxed attitude was the fact that three of us from the ward were taken by medical students to watch a film being shown within the hospital grounds. As we were teenage girls and the medical students were all male, we found this a very welcome distraction.

However, parental visiting was still severely limited and siblings were banned. Strangely, I was given permission to leave the ward briefly to attend a Welsh Choral concert in the Philharmonic Hall on a Saturday evening. My parents undertook to return me that night and to ensure I did not eat or drink anything except water.

Needless to say, the Mepacrine again failed to work its magic and I was again discharged. By this time, familiarity meant the worm had acquired a pet name. My school friends called it the very unimaginative 'Willy Worm'. More exciting to me was the worm's acquisition of a nationality. Since I could not have acquired anything so disgusting from home cooking, it was concluded that I had got it from eating dodgy pork while on a junior school trip to Bruges. Willy Worm was a foreign body in more ways than one. Willy Worm was Belgian.

The next worm onslaught was made after my sixteenth birthday. I was by then too old for Alder Hey and was classified as an adult with a tropical disease. As such I was to be treated in the tropical ward of the Royal Liverpool Hospital.

The port of Liverpool's international connections made the Liverpool School of Tropical Medicine a world-renowned institution. The school's Victorian red-brick building stood next door to the equally imposing Victorian red-brick hospital. Before I was admitted to the tropical ward, I was taken on a tour of the School of Tropical Medicine to reassure me, or so it was claimed.

The highlight of the tour was a walk through a passage-like room with a door at each end. Walking between the room's entrance and its exit, we were surrounded by wire netting. There was wire netting to the left of us, wire netting to the right of us, and wire netting above us. Behind the wire netting were locusts – thousands of them, looking like giant cockroaches with wings. It did not reassure me. It terrified me.

The tropical ward was a disappointment. Once, the port of Liverpool had attracted seafarers from all over the world, bringing with them exotic illnesses for treatment. By 1959 the women's tropical ward had shrunk to three beds in a general ward. The people occupying the beds were pleasant, but to my disappointment they were unable to come up with any interesting travellers' tales.

Before I was admitted to the Royal Liverpool Hospital, Dr Bruce, the lay reader at Holy Trinity Church, Wavertree, had slipped into my hand a small sheet of white paper with a Latin scientific name on it. 'Put this in your locker. If the Mepacrine doesn't work, ask them to give you these,' he said.

Dr Bruce had a surgery in Upper Parliament Street, Liverpool 8. He was a much-loved figure in that poor neighbourhood. When the Toxteth riots took place in 1981, it was noticeable that, while buildings surrounding it were wrecked by the mob, Dr Bruce's surgery was untouched.

The hospital staff were determined not to let my earlier reactions to Mepacrine defeat them. Once again I was told that it worked for the soldiers in the war, so it should work for me. The staff at the Royal planned to be a bit cleverer in the medicine's administration than Alder Hey had been. Following three days' starvation, a red rubber pipe was threaded up my nose, down the back of my throat and into my stomach. After the tube reached its destination, the Mepacrine was funnelled down the tube.

Once again, however, the Mepacrine did not work, so I produced Dr Bruce's piece of paper. The Latin on it referred to thirty large white tablets to be swallowed in two minutes flat. To my amazement, they worked. Thanks to Dr Bruce, I had been freed of Willy.

In the twenty-first century politicians of all parties vie with each other in expressing their love for the NHS. Nye Bevan, who put the 1948 Act establishing the NHS through Parliament, is regarded by many as a secular saint. It is hard, therefore, for people today to imagine just how fearful of health care many people were sixty years ago when the NHS was still in its infancy.

Part of the reason for their fear lay in the lack of available cures for many diseases. The use of antibiotics was still developing. Succumbing to an illness like rheumatic fever or pneumonia was a real fear. Children could be crippled by or die of polio, as the vaccine to prevent it was not invented until the mid-1950s.

After the war, there was no MMR jab; that vaccination was not introduced in the UK until 1988. When a child got measles, as it seemed most of us did, parents were terrified their child would die or go blind.

Systematic vaccination of teenage children with the BCG vaccination against TB was only introduced in 1953. That illness was also still greatly feared. Children knew that if you caught TB you would be sent away for months to a sanatorium where you had to sleep on balconies in the freezing cold, and you might even die. Curiously, my mother believed that TB had a hidden side effect. When a relative who developed the disease had lots of children, her fecundity was attributed by my mother, not to a failure to use birth control, but to a side effect of TB.

TB sufferers were not the only patients to be sent away. There were people who, suffering from schizophrenia or depression at a time when even less was known about mental illnesses than it is today, were 'put away' in large mental hospitals. Widespread ignorance of the causes of mental illness meant that having a family member put away in a hospital, like the huge Rainhill Asylum, was often seen as a cause of family shame rather than compassion.

But it was not just illnesses that prompted shame and fear. In the 1950s many Liverpool hospitals were housed in buildings that had previously been workhouses. When I had to go as an outpatient to Newsham General Hospital, my grandmother seemed more upset by *where* I was going than by my hideous warts. In her eyes, Newsham General Hospital was still Belmont Road Workhouse and my visits there shameful.

For me, the warts were a cause of humility. There were over two hundred on my hands – presumably a side effect of a weak immune system caused by Willy Worm. My teachers banned me from touching other children, particularly in PE lessons. I was also banned from cooking in domestic science lessons. In church, when readings from the Bible mentioned lepers, I felt I understood what they must have gone through. I sometimes felt all I needed was a bell, then I would have been able to wander around the school calling out: 'Unclean. Unclean.'

My regular visits to a clinic at Newsham General provided little consolation. Assorted members of the medical professions looked at my hands from a safe distance, and prescribed little brown bottles of ten per cent Formalin to smear on the offending lumps. The Formalin had no effect. Many people, including nurses at the clinic, suggested burying a piece of meat in a garden. The theory was that as the meat rotted, so the warts would rot. Everybody seemed to have a relative who had tried that cure with miraculous results, but it did not work for me.

Then, on one hospital visit, a miracle did occur. A handsome young doctor took hold of my hands, looked into my eyes and said: 'What a pity and you so pretty.' Within days, the warts had gone, every single one. Laying on of hands can sometimes work.

One old workhouse tradition that still operated in hospitals, even into the 1970s, was the key role of matron. In the workhouses, the matron had been supreme, and so it was for some time in the successor hospitals. But those matrons were not the matrons today's politicians mean when they talk nostalgically about 'bringing back matron'.

Old-fashioned matrons were in charge of a whole hospital and could be strict beyond belief. Nothing escaped their eyes. Nurses' behaviour and uniform, dirt in obscure places, behaviour of patients and visitors: all were subject to matron's scrutiny. When matron appeared on a ward, staff seemed to shudder and patients shared their concern. It was inevitable something had been done wrongly and matron would spot it.

On first being admitted to a hospital in those days, it was easy to assume that all doctors were men who could act as demigods with nobody above them. But it soon became clear that there was somebody above the men. Matrons were almost invariably women, and hospital doctors, I noticed, were almost invariably scared of them.

I saw the power of such women in action as a patient in Sefton General Hospital, which was housed in the former Toxteth Workhouse. A ganglion lump had grown on my wrist. Our GP prescribed dropping a large family Bible down on it hard so that it burst. We did not have a large family Bible, but an *Oxford English Dictionary* dropped from a height was seen as a suitable substitute. That did not work. An operation was prescribed.

The operation was early on a Friday morning. At lunchtime I went home. All weekend I was in agony. My fingers swelled until they could swell no more. My wrist throbbed. I cried and wanted to go back to hospital, but my father said I should grin and bear it. All weekend I suffered. On the Monday I returned to the hospital. A nurse took one look at my swollen hand and disappeared. It seemed that, while draining the ganglion, the surgeon had mistakenly severed a tendon in my arm.

The nurse returned with an older woman dressed in navy blue. 'Who did this?' the new arrival demanded in stentorian tones. She was told and then said, even more loudly: 'Come with me. We'll find him.' Terrified, I followed as she strode the long corridors looking for the offending surgeon. Nurses and doctors melted into the walls as she marched by.

Eventually we entered a ward. What a let-down. The man in question had gone on holiday. We marched back to outpatients, but I knew that when that surgeon returned he would be carpeted. Matron was a woman who pointed out men's mistakes in no uncertain terms.

Make do and mend

THE DRESS WAS pure white and beautiful. The silky skirt flowed from a bodice made from alternating strips of lace and shiny material. I put the dress on and twirled around. My parents admired the handiwork that had gone into making it, and I vainly admired myself wearing it.

The cast-off dress had been made for my honorary cousin, Judith, to wear for a Whit Sunday walk in Cheshire. It fitted me exactly. How kind it was of Auntie Dorothy to pass the dress on to me now that her daughter had grown out of it. Nobody minded that it was a hand-me-down, or that the strips of lace were included in the design only because there would not have been enough material to make a dress without them. Nobody commented adversely on the fact that part of the white material had once been one of Auntie Dorothy's undergarments.

This was soon after the war, and, even though clothes rationing ended in 1949, materials and clothing remained in short supply. Money to buy things was also often in short supply. Everybody I knew wanted to make the most of what they had. Recycling was intrinsic to our lives. I got the impression at the time that wool was a particularly precious commodity to be used, then reused.

Socks, jumpers, cardigans, pullovers, gloves and scarves were all made out of wool, and wool had a tendency to develop holes if it was worn a lot. My grandmother darning holes in my father's socks by the fireside in the evening was a regular family scene. The socks were quite thick. They would not stay up on my father's legs without the elasticised sock suspenders he used to hold them up. The socks frequently developed holes in the foot, particularly at the heel, but sometimes also where the rubber studs of the suspenders went through metal catches and pressed into the wool.

Another regular fireside scene involved rewinding wool from worn-out cardigans and jumpers. The garments were unpicked and the wool wound into small crinkly balls, then reused to make new Fair Isle patterned garments. The Fair Isle patterns were ideal for this type of recycling because they used so many different colours, and it was possible to adapt the colours used in the pattern of each garment according to the wool available.

If it was necessary to add to the recycled wool, looped skeins of new wool could be bought from a shop. Children were regularly asked to hold the skeins up between both arms, while an adult wound the wool into balls. It seemed impossible in those days to buy balls of wool.

Clothes made of wool were important in my early childhood not just because synthetics were not available, but also because we spent much of our lives trying to keep warm. There was no central heating and no double glazing to keep out draughts. Coal and wood fires heated most homes. Huddled in front of a coal fire, people could feel warm in front, but freezing cold on their backs. Cardigans and shawls were a comfort. In winter people regularly complained about having chilblains on their feet and hands.

Smoke from fires combined with the smoke from factories to pollute the atmosphere. When smoke and fog combined to create smog, the air could become so bad that schools were closed. Children were sometimes sent home from school while it was still just about possible to see where they were going.

My family was lucky. We had gas fires in our lounge and in two bedrooms, but there were coal fires in the morning room and dining room, and a coke fire in the large hall. At the start of each day, the coal and coke fires had invariably gone out and the gas fires still had to be lit. In winter, when we woke up, our big house was always very cold. There was often frost on the inside of the windows. The frost made beautiful rippling white patterns on the glass and could be scraped off with a fingernail.

Clothes were taken into bed to be warmed up before they were put on. Children learnt not just to dress themselves, but also to dress themselves under the bedclothes. This was trickier than it would be today because there were so many clothes to put on. People put layers of clothing on so they could keep warm.

Rationing and shortages meant parents encouraged their children to look after what clothes they had. My winceyette nightdresses and pyjamas were stored in a nightdress case. My handkerchiefs were kept in a box in a drawer so that moths could not get at them.

My grandmother was worried because she thought all our clothes might get eaten by moths, so she scattered Paradichlorobenzene mothballs in as many drawers and cupboards as she could find. Furs were thought to be particularly attractive to moths, but they were valued for the warmth they provided. In winter, when people who could afford them brought their furs out of storage, an aroma of mothballs floated round our church pews. This was in the days before political correctness, so nobody criticised the old ladies for wearing fur, and everybody was too polite to comment on the aroma of mothballs.

Rationing and the shortage of materials also affected bedclothes. To extend the life of our sheets my grandmother, like many others, side-to-middled thinning sheets. In other words, she cut the sheet in half and then hand sewed what had once been the sides together with a double seam. She then turned a hem at the sides on what had previously been the thinning or holed middle of the sheet. This sometimes meant our sheet edges were wonky as there was a limit to how well she could neaten off the holes.

Side-to-middled sheets were quite comfortable if they were made of cotton, but thick flannelette was a different matter. The thickness of the material meant that right in the middle of the bed was a raised lumpy line that could be very uncomfortable to lie on. Needless to say, all our sheets were flannelette.

Duvets had not been introduced into Britain. To keep warm, people piled as many woollen blankets as they could on their beds. Worn blankets, like sheets, were sometimes side-to-middled. We were better off than some families because a few of our blankets were very thick ones that my Belgian Auntie Yvonne had imported from her Delhayes relatives in Antwerp.

Cast-offs from Belgium were also used at our dinner table. We ate at a table clad in beautiful white tablecloths with napkins to match. My father was much amused by the contrast between the food we ate and the high quality of our table linen; he frequently referred with a smile to our 'double damask dinner napkins'. The tablecloths and napkins all had the Delhayes family's initials embroidered in red at a corner. Because they only used their initials, I never learnt the correct spelling of their surname.

It seemed obvious to me that my Auntie Yvonne's family at their home in Rue de la Constitution, Antwerp, were better off than we were at 30 Heathfield Road. The embroidered initials showed that, instead of washing things themselves, they had sent their table linen to a laundry. My impression of Belgium as a land of affluence was reinforced when my auntie started to travel regularly to Antwerp. She returned with Belgian chocolate biscuits and delicious chocolates, while sweet rationing was still in force in the UK.

The worst item of clothing for girls was the liberty bodice, a ridiculous and ridiculously named garment. Liberty bodices were sleeveless long vests made of stiff material and wool and were worn on top of proper vests. The bodices did not provide any liberty at all. They were very restrictive.

The really odd thing about liberty bodices was that, dangling from the bottom hem, were suspenders to hold up stockings. But young girls did not wear stockings. In summer we wore short socks. In winter we wore thick woollen three-quarter-length socks, held up by rings of elastic hidden under a turn down at the top of each sock. Our legs had red rings round them where the elastic pressed into the skin.

My father was always the first to wake in our house. He had to get to his office early and, until the mid-1950s, worked on Saturday mornings as well as Monday to Friday. As there was no central heating, he often woke to a cold house. After my grandmother died, every morning my father cleaned out three grates and reset the two coal fires with sheets of old newspaper rolled up into twists, firelighter and bits of wood with coal placed on top, all before he went to work. As far as possible, he used recycled wood.

Wood was a precious commodity. It was possible to buy small bundles for lighting the fire from Appleton's, the chandlers, at Penny Lane. If we could make do without such purchases, my family felt proud of themselves. Orange boxes were particularly valued as a source of firewood because they could be broken up, and the wood from one box would help light quite a few fires.

Many of the items imported into Britain through Liverpool docks were packed in wooden boxes or hessian sacking. Once they were emptied, the wooden boxes could be used for other purposes. I still have a small cabinet that my bonded warehouseman grandfather made with wood from the docks. It is used as a bedside table. It is not the most sophisticated item of furniture, but it has sentimental connections for me.

Wood was also recycled for use as toys. A common sight was children, pulled along by friends, sitting in carts made from old boxes attached to old pram wheels. These home-made carts could also be used to transport goods from shops and markets. I instinctively knew my parents would not let me have such a cart if I had had the courage to ask for one; such toys were for poor children.

Another way in which poor people carried goods home from the shops or market was in redundant prams. Those battered prams might be considered to be an early version of the now almost fashionable shopping trolleys; but in those days their use was regarded as 'common'.

My father used recycled wood to make toys. A particular success was a small rocking duck modelled on Donald Duck. One of the bedrooms in our Heathfield Road house was turned into a workroom with a workbench. There my father taught me to use a saw, chisel and vice to make small wooden boats from discarded wood.

A few days after my father's funeral my mother let me in to a secret: when I was about two years old, she had become pregnant for a second time, but the baby had been stillborn. That baby was a boy. I cannot know, but I suspect my father would have much preferred to instruct a son in the art of woodwork. However, my father never mentioned my stillborn brother to me, and my mother never mentioned the dead baby again. Both had been taught that it was a good thing to maintain what was then described as 'a stiff upper lip'.

The workroom walls were another example of making do in the aftermath of war. They were covered in a complex pattern of scraps of wallpaper left over from rolls used to decorate other rooms, together with prints of pictures from London's National Gallery. The prints had been taken from a book that was falling apart.

Paper of all sorts was precious. My mother kept a collection of cardboard boxes in a cupboard on the upstairs landing. They were a menace. Every time somebody opened the cupboard door, a pile of boxes fell out and hit them on the head. My father tried to stop my mother's box collecting. He suggested the habit had some deep Freudian significance, but she always insisted they would come in useful some day. Sometimes, but very rarely, one of them did.

Tissue paper, when we got hold of it, was also stored. Some of our early Christmas decorations were flowers made from recycled tissue paper. They were attached to twigs by strips of silver paper. There was delight when we were able to buy crinkly crêpe paper to make more paper flowers to add to them. However, our main Christmas decorations were small, second-hand black, white and brown flower sprays that Auntie Yvonne had brought back from Belgium.

Brown paper was also stored and reused. Parcels were wrapped in it ready for posting. Sellotape was not then in general use. Instead, parcels were tied together with string. My mother had a whole drawer of second-hand string saved for that purpose. She also squirrelled away knicker elastic, buttons and metal fastenings, including zips, poppers and hooks and eyes.

When a parcel was being wrapped up, my small child's hands were very useful in holding down the folded paper and the knots. My chief delight during parcel wrapping was the moment a stick of sealing wax was held over the string knots. I watched fascinated as my father held a flame to the wax and it melted, dripping red on to the knots and paper, thus sealing the parcel for the rigours of its journey.

It was not just materials that were recycled in the aftermath of the war. When we moved to Penny Lane, the neighbourhood's leftover food was still taken to a pig bin. Our local pig bin was on the pavement in Cassville Road outside the side of my Auntie Yvonne's house. The pig man collected the contents of the bin regularly. I could see our pig bin from our dining room window and much enjoyed watching the neighbours walking up to the bin, lifting the lid and emptying their scraps into it. My auntie was, however, delighted when pig bins, which had been encouraged as a wartime emergency, were abolished. Today they would probably be regarded as a health hazard.

Food was precious and bland, but as a child I did not know any different. Food rationing must have been much harder for adults who had known other things such as fresh fruit before the war. People sang a song called 'Yes! We Have No Bananas', but I had not seen a banana.

The first time I saw a banana was at the house of a fruit importer called Mr Elderton. I had been invited round to his family's house to admire the small egg their budgie – called

Joey and sold as male – had laid. They were delighted by this biological miracle. I was more interested in the banana I saw in their hall.

After regular imports of bananas were restored, my parents, walking along Otterspool Promenade, pointed out with awe the Fyffes' banana boats once again heading up river for Garston docks. The banana boats' return to the Mersey seemed somehow to them a confirmation that the misery of war and its aftermath were really over.

Cherries were also a rarity. The first time I saw a cherry I was eleven and in Bruges, Belgium, on a trip there with Mosspits Lane Junior School. The cherries were displayed on an outdoor stall. We knew they were cherries from pictures, but we had never seen or tasted any in Liverpool. Excitedly we bought a lot and planned a midnight feast at 9pm. They were delicious, particularly the dark red ones.

That school trip was quite an adventure. We were only eleven years old. Infrastructure had not recovered from the war, and transport was slow. The steam trains and cross-Channel ferries were very basic. One day we travelled by coach from Bruges to the port of Zeebrugge. We walked along a promontory out to sea. I wondered vaguely why our teachers were so quiet as we looked at the water. I did not think that they might have served in the war, or that some of their friends and families might have died nearby in the fighting.

That day nobody mentioned the role of the two historic Mersey ferries, *Daffodil* and *Iris*, in the First World War raid on Zeebrugge. The raid involved sinking old cruisers to block the port exit so that German vessels could not use it. The ferries' action led to their being awarded the title Royal: a title that I took for granted as a child, but was really unique.

I suspect the teachers did not mention that event, or the ferries' role in evacuating Dunkirk during the Second World War, because Liverpool had suffered so much from German bombing and they wanted to protect us.

Our teachers probably thought we were too young and

impressionable for the reality of war. If they did, they were right. When we visited the Basilica of the Holy Blood in Bruges, we got a bit upset at the idea of a cathedral being named after blood, but an art gallery's picture of somebody being skinned alive was worse. That painting was too much for one of the boys in our party. He rushed out of the gallery and was sick in the square outside.

In travelling to Belgium so soon after the war and at such a young age, we children from Mosspits Lane School were very lucky, but we were not aware of that fact. We were suspicious of the pea soup served at almost every meal and mused darkly about it being the same colour as the green algae-covered canal adjacent to our hotel. Did the hotel, we wondered, have a pea soup pipeline from the canal to its kitchen? However, like rationing, making do and mending, and the limited choice of food and toys, we accepted our first foreign trip, including the pea soup, as a natural part of our young lives.

Today, when I hear environmentalists talking of recycling as some sort of innovative practice, I am tempted to point out that there is nothing new about it at all. 'Make do and mend', which seemed a natural thing to do in the 1940s and 1950s, was really just recycling.

Being Welsh

I ALWAYS KNEW I was Welsh. That was perhaps odd because my parents and, as far as I know, all my grandparents were born in England – in Liverpool to be precise. However, tales of Wales were part of family folklore.

My maternal grandmother told me that her great-, or her great-great-grandmother had been a white Welsh witch, prescribing herbal cures in the countryside. My mother vehemently denied this, but both agreed that at one point a poor young girl relative had been denounced from a Welsh chapel pulpit for promiscuity and travelled to Liverpool to escape village wrath. Because I never asked, I will never know who the often-referred-to Jinny Bryntirion was, or in what way my mother was related to the woman who had a scandalous affair with a window cleaner somewhere around Prestatyn.

My mother's favourite childhood photograph was taken on St David's Day. For it, she was dressed in Welsh costume, complete with tall black hat. She often referred fondly to two Welsh uncles who, on emigrating to Australia because there were no jobs for them in Wales, had given her the pet canary they had taken down the coal mine with them. There was talk of another jobless relative who, in search of work, had walked to Liverpool from Denbigh, a town we sometimes visited to see other family members who lived there on the square. He had had to walk all that way because he had almost no money.

In my childhood Liverpool was known as the capital of north Wales. Every Thursday was Welsh day. It was the day people from north Wales travelled to the city centre by rail, coach and car to visit relatives and to shop.

There were many Welsh chapels scattered around the city. The large Heathfield Road Welsh Presbyterian chapel at

Penny Lane, with its minister's house and its Sunday school in Auckland Road, was at the bottom of our road. Built in 1926, the chapel was demolished in 2011. Its very size – it could accommodate a congregation of 750 – was an indicator of just how many Welsh people lived in our neighbourhood. Every Sunday the language heard on the streets was almost entirely Welsh as the congregation stood chatting on street corners after chapel.

I was told that the first owner of the five-bedroom end-terrace house in which we lived was a Welsh builder. He had built the house for himself and his family. The same man had also built the rows of terrace houses leading off Heathfield Road. I concluded the builder must have been quite affluent because, when we moved into the house, the main reception rooms and the bedrooms each had a bell push by their fireplace to summon our non-existent maid from her work in the morning room at the back of the house.

Many Welsh people lived in the terraces off Heathfield Road. They included a group of Welsh-speaking boys of whom I was not enamoured. When my mother went out and locked my friend Mary and me in the backyard to play with our stamp collections, the Welsh-speaking boys tried to climb over the wall from the back entry with the aim of scattering our stamps around the yard.

As a child I wanted to attend Heathfield Road Welsh chapel, but my father would not let me. He opposed the idea, not because I did not speak Welsh – I could have learnt by going to the chapel – but because speaking Welsh was seen by his generation as a liability. People thought it might hold you back in your career. I was sometimes envious of my friend, Anne Griffiths, who won lots of prizes at the chapel Sunday school, and whose father was a chapel elder.

When we were children Anne's father was very strict, particularly about Sunday observance. No Sunday newspapers were allowed in his house. He said that reading them was a sin. I could never understand why he did not mind reading

Monday's papers, which were written and printed on the Sabbath.

There was also a Welsh chapel ban on alcohol in Anne's house. This was particularly unfortunate the day, aged eighteen, she won a bottle of wine at the Liverpool Show. Getting that bottle to my house from Wavertree Mystery was a major challenge. It was not just Anne's father's wrath we feared, there was also the problem of the many members of the chapel's congregation who might spot us en route.

Anne stuffed the wine bottle inside her cardigan and we travelled furtively along the back entries until we reached the backyard of my house. We hid the bottle in the washhouse, and then confessed its acquisition to my parents. They were amused and invited Anne to Sunday lunch, at which we all had a glass of her wine.

As a sociologist, I put my feeling of Welsh identity down to the fact that my maternal grandmother, who lived with us for of most of my childhood, was very conscious of her family roots in Wales. Until her death, when I was in my mid-teens, my grandmother, not my mother, was in charge of daily household arrangements.

Grandma could be a bit extreme in her views on Welshness. She banned me from playing 'God Bless the Prince of Wales' on the piano, and maintained that Caernarfon, not Cardiff, was the capital of Wales. She explained that Caernarfon had only lost its capital status thanks to an English trick on the Welsh, when a baby had been foisted on them. The English, who had had the temerity to claim the baby was the Prince of Wales, had dangled that baby from the battlements of Caernarfon castle.

Each St David's Day, Grandma would muse about whether the leek should be the only national symbol of Wales. Her grandfather had told her that the use of the daffodil was really part of another English plot against the Welsh. My mother ignored my grandmother's concerns and always bought daffodils for the house on 1 March.

Despite these views, my grandmother did not attend the

Welsh chapel at the bottom of our road, preferring to accompany the rest of the family to an Anglican church. Having grown up as a Welsh Methodist, she had never been confirmed or even baptised as a member of the Church of England, but she always took Anglican Communion when it was offered. That was against Anglican rules at the time, but that did not bother her. My grandmother did not lie about her status to the Anglican clergy; she just did not tell them she was an interloper.

Grandma adopted a similar approach to the Conservative Party. Her social life centred on the weekly whist drives at the Waverton Conservative Club in Church Road. At election time, she always accepted the Conservatives' offer of a lift in a car to the Penny Lane polling station in Elm Hall Drive. At the polling station, she would get out of the Conservative car, enter the polling station and vote Labour. She never told the Conservatives how she voted. Her defence to a family charge of duplicity was that it was a secret ballot.

From the first-floor workroom window near the back of our Heathfield Road house we could see Wales. We used the view as a weather forecast. We could see Moel Famau, the highest mountain in the Clwydian range, particularly clearly if it was going to rain. Moel Famau was an important part of our lives. Camping in the Vale of Clwyd in the 1930s, my parents had taken their Life Boys up to its summit and photographed them on top of the ruined monument that was built to commemorate George III's Golden Jubilee, and so is called the Jubilee Tower.

My Auntie Fran, a teacher, regularly took children to Colomendy, a camp in the shadow of Moel Famau. The camp was popular with Liverpool schoolchildren and many got their first experience of the countryside staying there.

Buying a car gave our family new freedom. Before my father owned a car, most of our trips to Wales had been by rail: on holiday to Colwyn Bay or Aberystwyth (changing at Rock Ferry, Gobowen and Oswestry), or by bus to stay on a farm called Min-y-Clwyd in Ruthin.

After my father bought a car, he felt he could drive

anywhere; but our principal destinations for days out were in Wales. We drove to north Wales to visit relatives in Denbigh, to pick bilberries on Llandegla Moor and to buy eggs near Ruthin.

Sometimes in summer we bought fish and chips in Ruthin and then took them, in their vinegar soaked newspaper, to eat sitting on the grass above the high road that skirts the side of Moel Famau, between Ruthin and Mold. The view of the Vale of Clwyd from the mountain made it worth waiting for the chips. Sheep often came up to us and seemed curious about what we were doing. Sometimes, too, I picked purple heather or looked for forget-me-nots in the rills at the side of the road. This was all before the area became a country park and when not many people had cars. Then there were no explanatory signs on Moel Famau, no litter and no traffic noise, but lots of bleating and birdsong.

My favourite holiday place was Penrallt, an old house my father learnt about from the advertisements in the *New Statesman*. The moment he read the words: 'Hill lovers offer hospitality in remote farmhouse,' he wanted to go there.

Penrallt was indeed remote. It was on the shores of Llyn Geirionydd, then a place of peace and tranquillity. I shared a bedroom with Ruth Bonner, a daughter of the owners. Together we took her pony along the lakeside. After opening and closing various gates, we explored, from above ground, the disused mineshafts that littered the area. Sometimes I swam in the dark waters of the lake. It was cold and felt very deep.

People sometimes warn: never go back. How right they are in the case of Llyn Geirionydd. For some strange reason, the powers that be in the Snowdonia National Park have given permission for waterskiing and powerboating to take place on that once peaceful lake.

Among the highlights of the Liverpool Welsh community during my childhood was the annual series of concerts given by the Liverpool Welsh Choral Union at the Philharmonic Hall. The choir was then very large, occupying almost every seat behind the Liverpool Philharmonic Orchestra. People came from all over north Wales to listen to the choir singing oratorios, and sometimes opera scores. Each year my parents bought tickets for the Welsh Choral's series of concerts. The first time I went we sat in the stalls; but soon we migrated to a box.

Sitting in the front box, I was squirmingly conscious of my blue and beige tweed suit, the hat that pinched my head, and the fact that I was in full view of school friends and schoolteachers sitting in the balcony. However, the intervals could be even more embarrassing, particularly when my parents decided to frequent the bar next to the ladies' lavatory and have an alcoholic drink. They did not seem to care that we were at a Welsh Choral concert, or that most of the audience were keen chapelgoers who thought alcohol the work of the Devil.

Hardly anybody went into the bar at Welsh Choral concerts, so whenever my parents visited the bar for a drink I was deeply embarrassed. Children were not allowed in licensed premises in those days, so my parents left me standing alone, outside the bar, waiting for them. Desperately, I tried to convey the impression that I was not with the drinkers, but was instead waiting for somebody to come out of the nearby lavatories.

Sometimes at Welsh Choral concerts my father would say at the start of the interval: 'Let's go and see Flash Harry.' We would then proceed from our box to the green room where the conductor, a very tall man, would bend down and say 'Hello' to me. The very tall man was the great conductor Sir Malcolm Sargent. He was Principal Conductor of the Liverpool Philharmonic Orchestra between 1942 and 1948, and continued to be associated with the Liverpool Welsh Choral after he left the city.

Liverpool was very proud of its orchestra's long history and saw Manchester's Hallé as an upstart. When the Liverpool Philharmonic Society was granted the title 'Royal' in 1957, my father told me a telegram was sent to the Hallé saying simply,

'How's the Hallé?' The telegram was signed 'Royal Liverpool Philharmonic Orchestra', the emphasis being on the Royal.

One of our first journeys in the new family car was to Lake Vyrnwy. The lake and its surrounding estate were then owned by Liverpool Corporation. The Corporation built a dam across the valley in the 1880s and the first water flowed from the lake to the city in 1891. The reservoir was needed for the city's ever increasing population: many of them emigrants from Wales. Its creation involved flooding a valley and drowning a village called Llanwddyn.

Lake Vyrnwy is surrounded by trees, mostly pines. I was told that, when pines were first planted around the lake, the Corporation failed to include gaps between the rows of trees. This meant it was difficult to get damaged trees, or chopped down ones, out. But by the time my parents took me there, that mistake had been rectified and the City Council was working with the Forestry Commission.

On our visit we drove around the edge of the lake, looked at photograph albums containing sepia pictures of the men who had built the dam, met people working on the estate, had refreshments at what is now the Lake Vyrnwy Hotel, and admired the beautiful water tower which juts out into the lake.

To my great excitement, a door in the water tower was unlocked for us and we were taken inside to see the filters. It was pitch-black in the tower. When a light was switched on I saw a most amazing sight: blind trout swimming in the water at the top of the tank that housed the filters. Surprisingly their skins were not mottled and brown, but white. The fishes' eyes were covered by a white membrane. Somehow the trout, or their ancestors, must have got into the tower as eggs, hatched and grown into fish. I was told that the lights in the tower were hardly ever switched on. This meant that, being constantly in the dark, the fish had become white-skinned and lost their eyesight.

My father was quite emotional about Lake Vyrnwy. His

mother's family had left Wales to seek work in Liverpool. Many Welsh people, who had moved from Wales to Liverpool in search of jobs, derived benefit from Lake Vyrnwy's water. But a village had been flooded to create the lake and other Welsh people had lost their land and their homes. Yet still Liverpool did not have enough water. Another valley was to be flooded and another village, this time the village of Capel Celyn, was to be drowned.

Liverpool City Council debated the flooding of the Tryweryn Valley and the drowning of Capel Celyn to create a new reservoir. That day my father returned home from the Council meeting in the Town Hall. I came out of the lounge, where I had been playing the piano, just as he closed the vestibule door. He said nothing, but stood totally still in the hall. I saw tears in his eyes and, being only thirteen, did not know how to react. My mother went to comfort him.

Eventually my father told us that people in the public gallery of the Town Hall had stood up and sung the Welsh national anthem. They were protesting against the flooding of the valley. He was sitting on the dais, facing the public gallery and the councillors and aldermen. He knew that, as a council official, he must not show emotion, but the singing had almost been more than he could cope with.

Years later there was a drought and the broken outlines of buildings, once part of the drowned Capel Celyn, were exposed by the low water. My father drove my mother and me to Tryweryn. We stood side by side at the lake edge viewing the crumbled remains of the drowned village. Deep in thought, we said nothing.

Foreign relations

THE BATHROOM REEKED of a combination of Evening in Paris and 4711 scents. My father had returned from the German city of Cologne with the biggest bottle of 4711 Eau de Cologne available. First he gave the bottle to my mother, but she rejected it because she preferred her traditional Coty L'Aimant. Then she handed the bottle over to me. Excitedly I poured the contents of the bottle of Evening in Paris, given to me at Christmas and no longer wanted, down the lavatory, and then poured a generous amount of 4711 into my bath. That was why the bathroom had such a curious aroma.

The huge bottle of 4711 had been presented to my father by Dr Max Adenauer, Cologne City Director between 1953 and 1965 and son of the West German Chancellor Konrad Adenauer. The occasion was a town twinning civic visit to Cologne by the Lord Mayor of Liverpool, accompanied by assorted civic dignitaries.

The highlight of this visit, for my father, was the moment he was challenged by customs officers at the airport on the civic party's return. 'Anything to declare?' they asked. 'Only this,' replied my father, pulling out the city's heavy, solid gold Lord Mayoral chain with its Liver bird pendant. He was relieved to have got it back safely to the UK and not to have had it stolen from him in Germany.

In the aftermath of the Second World War, European local government was very keen on town twinning or 'jumelage', as the Council of European Municipalities called it. There was a feeling that if people from different European countries got to know each other socially, there would not be another war. Liverpool had experienced heavy German bombing during the war. It therefore seemed to be a perfect idea to twin with the city of Cologne, a city that still bore the scars of heavy British bombing.

Cologne was not the only city Liverpool twinned with. Because they were both large ports, it was agreed that the French city of Marseille and Liverpool should twin. My mother accompanied my father on a civic twinning visit there and greatly enjoyed herself. She liked the French politician Gaston Defferre, who at the time was Mayor of Marseille, and particularly enjoyed sightseeing when, in a huge car and accompanied by police outriders, they were shown a view of the city and its docks from high on a hill overlooking the port.

Another city Liverpool twinned with during my youth was the Black Sea port of Odessa, then in Russia but currently in Ukraine. According to my father the civic visit there was interesting, but not fun. The civic party were worried they were being watched. My father copied a spy book trick and stuck a hair, one of the few he had left, on the opening crack at the side of his suitcase. The spy book theory was that if the hair was not there when he returned to his room, he would know somebody was spying on him and had opened his case. When he got back, the hair had disappeared; thus the members of the visiting civic party were confirmed in their paranoia.

The widespread post-war belief that development of personal friendships across European borders would promote peace and prevent future wars meant children were often encouraged by their secondary schools to have foreign penfriends. A few of these friendships survive to this day, but most dwindled away.

My French penfriend was a disaster. I was a city girl; she was a child of French peasants. Early in our correspondence, she came to stay with us in Liverpool. When, visiting a farm in north Wales, she entered the cowshed and promptly pulled her knickers down to pee with gusto, I immediately realised our friendship was doomed. We had nothing in common. I cannot even remember her name and never returned her visit.

Possibly learning from such experiences, the staff at

Aigburth Vale High School tried hard to match the backgrounds of our next lot of penfriends. This time, we were to become friends with Swedish girls. That was much better. Ingrid Bernerup came to stay with us and, as well as seeing the sights of Liverpool, we went to London. Going round the Tower of London, my mother pointed at a suit of armour and asked us enthusiastically: 'Doesn't this make history come alive?' In unison Ingrid and I replied: 'No.' At that moment we two girls had much in common: we were both very bored teenagers.

Ingrid Bernerup's parents owned a farm at Stora Bernstorp near Malmö. Walking on boards through a shed above hundreds of pigs, their snouts turned up to look at us, was an amazing experience. I was scared I would fall down into the pens and be eaten. More relaxed were the weeks I spent with Ingrid's family at their holiday home on the Swedish south coast.

Ingrid's parents were very kind, though I still wonder what they thought of my explanation for the cause of a very large graze on my knee. It must have been hard for them to believe I had merely fallen over in the road. A much more believable and truthful explanation was that I had fallen off the luggage rack of Ingrid's friend Sven's moped, while crossing railway tracks at speed. But Ingrid had warned me against making a confession. The practice of luggage rack riding was not only dangerous, as we had found out, but also illegal.

I never met my third penfriend: an American called Michelle. In the 1950s foreign travel was costly and very limited. It never occurred to me that I might travel to America or Michelle travel to Liverpool. However, the subscription to *Life* colour magazine that her parents took out for me was a useful education, not only about America but also about aesthetics. Its photographs, many of which are now available on the Internet, were outstanding.

Today, when foreign countries are mentioned, children can conjure up much better images than my generation could. Most children of my generation did not have a television until well into their teens, not even a black-and-white one. Colour printing was limited, so most of the printed pictures we saw were in black and white, which was why the vivid colour photographs in *Life* magazine seemed so exciting to me.

One foreign country that loomed quite large in my childhood was Australia. It was the era of the £10 Poms. There was a lot of chatter about people moving to start a new life in Australia through a system of assisted migration. My mother pointed out that going to Australia from Liverpool was not new. Lots of Liverpudlians had left Liverpool bound for Australia before the Second World War. Two of her uncles had gone as unassisted migrants; they were the miners who had left her the canary they had used to detect gas in the mines.

In my second year at grammar school, we entered a seemingly endless study of Australia in geography lessons. Week after week, we traced the outline of that island on crisp Bronco lavatory paper, transferred it to exercise books and then marked in things like rainfall, cities and fences. We traced Australia's outline so often that I, quite wrongly, began to feel a sneaking dislike of the country and a great hatred of the study of geography.

Africa was different. It was nearer. Somehow I always felt that one day I would visit that continent. In the 1950s Liverpool's churches and chapels were full; and many congregations still enthusiastically sponsored missionaries to go to foreign countries and spread the word of Christianity. The church I attended, Holy Trinity Wavertree, supported the Church Missionary Society (CMS), a missionary organisation that was then very active in Africa. One of the countries in which CMS missionaries were active was Uganda. A missionary called Margaret Gurney Champion, a distant relative of the great prison reformer Elizabeth Fry, visited Holy Trinity. She told us about her work at Gayaza High School for Girls, which is the oldest girls' school in Uganda. Through this connection, people involved with the school came to stay with us in Liverpool, and my friends and I began to learn about Africa.

The first Ugandan to visit us was Christine Batuwade. She was studying at the C F Mott Teacher Training College, which was then in Prescot. When I was seven, walking up Heathfield Road, Christine warned me about the danger of hippos.

Apparently, one day a man was walking along a road when a hippo chased him. He started to run to get away from the hippo. But the hippo could run faster than the man and soon caught up with him. The hippo chopped the man exactly in half. The amazing thing was not that the man's body was chopped exactly in half, it was that the man's legs carried on running along the road, while his top half lay at the side of the road saying: 'The hippo got me. The hippo got me.' It was not clear to me, or to Christine, what then happened to the hippo, but the moral of her tale was clear to me: be very wary of hippos at Penny Lane.

This scary picture of Africa lost some of its credibility the day my parents took Christine and me to visit Chester Zoo. Christine thought it really interesting, particularly the lions. I was disappointed to discover that, there in Chester Zoo, she was seeing a lion for the first time. Until that day I had imagined Africa to be full of hippos and lions.

Standing, sixty years later, near the neglected memorial to the explorer John Hanning Speke by the source of the Nile, I did not give a thought to hippos, lions, or even crocodiles. The atmosphere was too peaceful to worry about such things. I did, however, wonder vaguely if John Hanning Speke and Liverpool's Speke Hall were in any way connected. Apparently not.

Some time after Christine returned to Gayaza High School, one of its former schoolgirls came to Liverpool to study physiotherapy. My parents welcomed her into our home. Marion was five years older than me. She became the big sister I had yearned for; and I became another little sister for her to care about. Over half a century later, that honorary family relationship has not changed.

Through Marion, my parents also met Noerine Kaleeba and

Mary Lukubo, but by the time they arrived in Britain, I was living in London. Noerine and Mary trained as physiotherapists in Oswestry and spent some of their free time staying with my parents in Liverpool, and visiting me in Westminster. Later, tragedy struck when it was discovered that Noerine's husband had caught AIDS from a blood transfusion after a traffic accident. He eventually died.

Miraculously, Noerine did not catch the disease; but it transformed both Noerine's and Mary's lives. They gave up being physiotherapists. Through the creation of TASO (The AIDS Support Organisation) in Uganda, they devoted their energies to tackling AIDS and educating people about the disease.

Another former Gayaza High School student who travelled to Liverpool to study was Mary Kajabwangu. She planned to become a nurse. She was only eighteen when my parents were asked to keep an eye on her. Soon after her arrival in Liverpool, she visited them for tea. The next thing they knew, she was a patient in Fazakerley Hospital. Mary had TB. She must have arrived in Britain with the disease.

My parents and I went to visit Mary in the hospital. She was the tallest woman I had ever seen. The hospital bed was too small for her. Her legs hung out over its end and her very large feet jutted out from under the sheets. Having only recently arrived in a strange country to study and suddenly finding herself in hospital with a possibly fatal disease, Mary, despite her size, seemed to us to be just a frightened little girl.

A few weeks later, the hospital discovered that Mary had become pregnant almost immediately after she arrived in Liverpool. She was very young, distraught and ashamed. My parents supported her. When Robin, her baby, was baptised, they became his godparents. Eventually Robin, by then a toddler, was sent to Uganda to be cared for by people there, while his mother continued her studies in Liverpool. My father and I took him to London Heathrow for onward transportation to the Ugandan capital, Kampala.

After she qualified as a nurse and returned to Uganda, my parents lost touch with Mary Kajabwangu and their Liverpool-born godson. Then, years after my father's death, a man phoned my mother. He said he was her godson from Uganda and was in London. Robin then went to stay with my mother overnight in Liverpool. The trusting little toddler had grown into a giant man. He was so strong he could hold up the back of a small car while its wheel was changed; but, emotionally, he was as vulnerable as a child.

Mary had been a far from ideal mother. Robin told us that in his early teens he returned home from school one day to discover his mother and half-brothers had left without telling him where they were going. The young boy went wild, sleeping where he could: in trees, in discos, anywhere. Then somebody recognised Robin on the streets of Jinja, a town in the south of Uganda, and kindly took him back with her to work in Kampala.

But Robin wanted to know about his roots. How exactly had he come to be born in Liverpool? What was Liverpool like? Who was his father? What were his godparents like? He wanted to return to Britain to answer these questions.

At first the British High Commission in Kampala refused his application for a British passport due to lack of evidence about his birth. His mother's flit had left Robin with almost nothing. He did not have a birth certificate and did not know how he could prove he had been born in Liverpool.

Then a friend remembered she had a photograph from Robin's Liverpool baptism. He took it to the High Commission as part of his proof of identity. Before returning the photograph to its owner, Robin copied it. Taken at the porch of a Liverpool church, the photograph shows Robin in my mother's arms, with my father looking on.

When Robin eventually arrived in London, he showed the photograph around, asking: 'Do you know these people?' Eventually he went to a Citizens Advice Bureau. After checking on Sir Stanley Holmes and finding he had died, they told him his godparents were both dead. Yet Robin did not give up his search for a link to his short Liverpool life.

One day, at a party in east London, he showed the photograph to somebody who said: 'That's Uncle Stan and Auntie Doris.' Thus Robin, after over twenty years, was able to be reunited with his Liverpool godmother. He never discovered his father's name or even his nationality because his mother never told anyone who had made her pregnant. But, thanks to that treasured photograph, Robin found people who had known and loved him from the time he was born.

Later, in south London, Robin married Kathy. Their first child, Christopher, was baptised in St Margaret's, Westminster, by the then Speaker's chaplain, Canon Donald Gray, a former Rector of Liverpool and a family friend. My husband, Denzil Davies, who had been best man at the wedding, became Christopher's godfather and I became his godmother. Their second child, Christine, was also baptised at St Margaret's with my daughter as a godmother. My son and his wife became godparents to their third child, Kathryn Mary.

Before his mother died Robin, with his wife Kathy's loving support and understanding, felt able to take Christopher and Christine to Uganda to meet her. In baptising his third child, Kathryn Mary, with her Ugandan grandmother's name, Robin showed an understanding and forgiveness of his late mother many of us would find difficult.

In 2011, Robin died aged forty-six. The first photograph on the Order of Service for his funeral in Peckham, London, had been taken at a Liverpool church porch. It was the treasured baptismal picture of baby Robin lying in my mother's arms with my father looking on.

The quality of Mersey

A SHINY BRASS pole gleamed at the centre of the hole in the first floor of Hatton Garden Fire Station. A uniformed fire officer explained that when the alarm went off in the station, the firemen would leap up and slide down the pole. That was the quickest way to reach the fire engines below, and much quicker than using the stairs.

Marcus, my honorary Auntie Dorothy and Uncle Ronnie's son, for whose education my father had arranged our visit to Liverpool's Fire Service's headquarters, was delighted to be invited to wrap his arms and legs round the pole and slide down. One moment, he was on the first floor with us. Then whoosh, he went down. The pole was very slippery. How I longed to follow Marcus down the pole. I asked to do so, but was told that sliding down poles was not what young girls did. It was not ladylike.

After the rest of the party had walked downstairs, the fire officer talked to us about the city's fireboat. It was called the *William Gregson* after a Labour Alderman who was Chairman of the City Council's Watch Committee when the boat was launched.

The Corporation kept the fireboat on the river to fight fires aboard ships and in the docks. In 1960, some years after our visit to the fire service headquarters, the *William Gregson* was used to pump river water by relay to put a fire out in Hendersons, the downtown department store. That fire particularly shocked my school friends and me because a woman who had been our form prefect was among the dead.

The fire officer told us that the fireboat's crew sometimes fished bodies out of the Mersey. When people fell from a dockside, a boat or the Pier Head, they were most unlikely to survive. But the fallers did not drown. There was no time for that. They were poisoned before they could drown, so polluted was the river in those days.

This information prompted my father to misquote Shakespeare: 'The quality of Mersey is not strained,' he said. Marcus and I did not find that funny. However, if not straining, the Mersey water needed something doing to it. It was filthy and sometimes stank when you got near it. The problem was not just human sewage; all sorts of industries upstream pumped their polluting waste into the River Mersey.

When my family moved to Penny Lane, Liverpool was still a very lively port. Ferries criss-crossed the river between the city and the Wirral. The Irish boat and the Isle of Man boat waited for passengers at the Pier Head. Vessels laden with goods were unloaded in the many docks. Passenger liners entered dry docks for refit. Fussy, yellow-funnelled tugs, hooting messages to each other, busily escorted larger vessels into docks. Ships were still being built at Cammell Laird at Birkenhead.

Arriving at Lime Street Railway Station, visitors to the city were immediately made aware of the fact that the city was a very active port. A very tall man in green uniform, who seemed to my child's eyes to be a giant, stood on the station concourse shouting repeatedly: 'Irish boat, Irish boat.'

My parents were more interested in the Isle of Man boat. They had sailed on an Isle of Man boat to that island for a holiday in Port Erin just before the war. When I was baptised at St Michael-in-the-Hamlet church, Toxteth, they asked their friend Lena Callister to be my godmother. She was active in the Liverpool Manx Society. I was very impressed that my godmother spoke Manx.

In those days the connection between the island and Liverpool was close, and the Liverpool Manx Society had quite a large membership. I was not, however, interested in hearing about the Manx Society's activities. I wanted to know the secret of my godmother's mother's hair. She seemed to be a very old lady and her hair was so clean and shining white. One day, I plucked up the courage to ask her how she managed to get her hair to glow. She explained she only washed it once a year. The rest of the time she just polished it with a silk stocking. I still find that almost unbelievable.

When I was in my teens, my parents became nostalgic about the Isle of Man. They decided to take me with them to revisit Port Erin, where they had stayed early in their marriage. Once the Manx boat reached the Mersey Bar, the sea became very rough. We were banned from standing outside on the deck. Waves smashed over the side and could have swept us away. A lot of passengers were seasick.

As the boat pitched from side to side, I began to understand why there were so many wrecks in the Irish Sea. They included the Liverpool-Isle of Man mail boat, the *Ellan Vannin*, about which the Liverpool folk group, The Spinners, sang a sad folk song. Ellan Vannin is the Manx name for the Isle of Man. The boat named *Ellan Vannin* sank near the Mersey Bar lightship during a storm in 1909, while taking mail from the island to Liverpool.

Our visit to Port Erin took place at a time when my mother was still convinced I would one day swim the English Channel. In pursuit of this dream, my parents hired a rowing boat and we set out towards a headland on one side of that bay.

Near Bradda Head, I dropped overboard then swam round Port Erin Bay to a breakwater near the opposite headland. I wonder now who was the more foolhardy, my parents in a small rowing boat in the waters of the Irish Sea, or me. During our Isle of Man holiday, my father also arranged a private visit to Liverpool University's Fisheries Research Station, which stood on one side of Port Erin Bay and where a great deal of work was done on things like monitoring Irish Sea herring stocks. Alas, the university closed the station in 2006.

Activity on the Mersey could be heard from our Heathfield

Road house. Each day, the one o'clock gun reverberated over the city to remind dockers and other citizens of the time. Hearing it, people with watches would instinctively check they had the correct time. When a ship was launched, other ships on the river hooted with delight as it travelled down the slipway. At midnight on New Year's Eve, the sound of vessels on the river hooting loudly heralded a new year.

As the 1950s progressed, river traffic decreased. My father, son of an unemployed docker, worried that the Port of Liverpool was dying. He would comment adversely on the Port of Southampton. With its four tides a day, compared with Liverpool's two, that port was draining the lifeblood from our city.

However, it was not just Southampton's four tides a day that was leading to the decline in shipping on the Mersey. Containerisation was changing the way cargoes were carried and so the nature of port work was also changing. Rather than dockers going down into the hold of vessels to haul up crates and sacks, as my grandfather had done, huge cranes began to lift containers from ship to dockside.

Trading patterns were also changing. Liverpool was in the wrong place. The city was further than Southampton from London and the south-east of England where Britain's population and wealth were increasingly focused. Liverpool faced Ireland and America rather than the growing markets in Europe. Moreover, Merseyside's dock workforce had a widespread reputation for being difficult and willing to strike at a moment's notice.

The decline of the docks meant that something needed to be done to bring new jobs to the city. Eventually, the Ford Motor Company started negotiations with Liverpool Corporation to build a factory at Halewood, near the council estate at Speke. My father was delighted and closely involved. Frequent visits to Hale village followed. At one point my parents even considered moving to live in Hale lighthouse on the banks of the Mersey. That prospect ended when they discovered the lighthouse was just outside the city boundary, because in those days local authority chief officers were required to live within the geographical area they served. However, for a few years my parents still drove to Hale to buy country bunches of flowers from outside cottage doors.

In the middle of the negotiations with Ford, my father drove my mother and me, in our blue Hillman Minx car, through quiet country lanes to the edge of a field at Halewood. There he switched off the car engine. Quietly he told us that where we were sitting might become the site of a new car factory. Contracts had not yet been signed, but, if they were, the new factory would bring many greatly needed jobs to Liverpool. We sat in the car in silence listening to the birds and enjoying the quietness of the countryside. I saw tears gleaming in my father's eyes. I did not know if he was praying, but suspected he was.

While the docks near the city centre were still operating, my father took great delight in walking through them. The dock names – Canning, Herculaneum, Huskisson, Canada, Gladstone, Albert – rolled off his tongue. He was delighted when he found an old right of way through the docks; it was accessed via a dock gate. From time to time we would walk the right of way, just to prove we could. First we had to tell the policeman at the gate that we were exercising our right of way. Policemen stood at the dock gates to stop dockers taking things that were not theirs out of the docks. They sometimes seemed taken aback by our request to enter the docks and walk along the right of way, but they always let us in.

Warehouses towered above us as we walked through the docks. At one point the right of way involved crossing a bridge over the entrance to a dry dock. The walk was particularly exciting if a passenger liner was entering the dry dock for repairs and blocked our way because the bridge across the dock entrance from the river had swung aside to admit the vessel.

One day my parents and I went aboard the Elder Dempster

Lines ship, the *Apapa*. It was taking on passengers ready for its departure for Lagos, Nigeria. On board, we said a sad goodbye to my parents' Nigerian friends, and were introduced to a very tall man who, I was told, was the Lord Chief Justice of Nigeria. I worried that, as he was used to criminals, he might notice I had just purloined a ship's beer mat for my beer mat collection. Then the announcement: 'All ashore that's going ashore,' made my heart beat with fear. I had enjoyed being on the ship, but I did not want to go to Nigeria or have to be taken off by the pilot boat at the Mersey Bar.

The strangest vessel I encountered was the VA3 hovercraft that briefly travelled between Moreton on the Wirral and Rhyl. In 1962 my parents were due to be part of the civic party on that hovercraft's inaugural flight. I was home from university and invited to join them.

The flight was an odd experience. We flew above the waves to the edge of a beach on which a row of narrow planks had been placed on the sand. Then we walked, one behind the other, along the planks and up the beach away from the water. When we reached the top of the beach, we turned round and walked back again along the planks. At the time I was mesmerised by how out of place civic chains, men's formal suits and ladies' heeled shoes were on the sands. I hardly noticed that I had travelled on the first commercial passenger carrying hovercraft in the world.

In our childhood my friends and I spent quite a lot of time on the Mersey ferries. Going to Birkenhead by underground railway, or by bus or car through the Mersey Tunnel, was nowhere near as exciting as crossing the river by ferry. Today I find it hard to adjust to the idea that taking a ferry across the Mersey is no longer akin to taking a bus, but has become a tourist experience. It seems odd to me also that most people, who sing along to Gerry and the Pacemakers' song 'Ferry 'Cross the Mersey', cannot recall the days when the ferries were the water equivalent of buses and continually criss-crossed the river taking people to and from their daily work.

In my childhood taking the ferry combined practicality with pleasure. Depending on the tide, the floating landing stage would either be almost level with the Pier Head or sloping steeply downwards. The tide also affected the deck from which we got on or off the ferry.

We always sat on the top deck, but, as the ferry approached Birkenhead, we would try to guess at which deck level the gangway would connect boat and dry land. It seemed important to get near the right gangway exit. It was also important to sit down or hold on to something before the ferry went alongside because, despite the fenders that muffled any bump, passengers could still be jolted as ferry met landing stage.

Sometimes it was enough just to go back and forth on the ferry without getting off. My grandmother did that frequently; she claimed the sea air relieved her asthma. There was so much traffic to see on the river; each river crossing was different. Sometimes I would peep down into the ferry's engine room, in one of which the father of my chess-playing friends Joy and Bill worked. Smelling the oil and listening to the throbbing of the engine seemed very exciting.

I particularly enjoyed going on the ferry with my mother to visit Birkenhead Market. It was much more fun to get there by ferry, than to travel with her on the underground railway under the Mersey to Birkenhead's Hamilton Square Station. It also felt healthier; the underground always seemed to smell of oil, dust and smoke, whereas the river breezes wafted life into my lungs.

My mother thought the indoor part of Birkenhead Market better for dress and furnishing materials than Liverpool's St John's Market. I preferred the outdoor section of Birkenhead Market. If my mother had allowed me, I would have stood for hours listening to the patter of a man who sold china. My interest must have been noticeable because one day he paused, leant down from his platform and gave me a small china jug for free. It was chipped then, but I still have it; on the base is written: 'Canadian Pacific' and 'B.C. Coast Steamships'.

When we became teenagers, my school friends and I were allowed to go on the ferries by ourselves. Our teenage ferry journeys were almost invariably to New Brighton. Passing Mother Redcap's, a large building on the shore overlooking the river, we would remember tales of Mersey smugglers who were said to have used the house as a headquarters. There were supposed to be underground passages in the area, but we never knew anybody who had found one.

Fort Perch Rock at New Brighton was a mystery to us. It loomed above the rocks near where we sometimes paddled with our skirts tucked in our knickers. Though it had protected the Mersey since the days of Napoléon and operated as a battery during the war, it seemed empty and silent by the 1950s. Some years later a man my father knew bought the fort, and invited us to look around it. Inside, the building was as chaotic and neglected as I had expected, with old ropes, bits of metal and dark sticky stains everywhere. What repelled me most was the smell. The building reeked of the remains of oil, war and the River Mersey's past pollution, but I could see that Fort Perch Rock had potential and to be invited inside was exciting. I am glad it is now restored and others can visit it.

Before we were allowed to go there on our own, my parents sometimes took my friends and me to New Brighton on the ferry. There we tasted the delights of chocolate Kunzle cakes, served in a tea shop near the New Brighton Tower fairground. We were also frequently warned about the dangers of possible quicksand on beaches and the need to take care near the lighthouse and Fort Perch Rock.

My friend Mary and I loved going to the New Brighton fairground. We particularly enjoyed the Wall of Death: a circular pit around the walls of which motorbike riders sped, their bikes and bodies horizontal to a disappearing floor. We had acquired our interest in motorbikes from Mary's father and her cousins. They sometimes took us to watch Speedway racing at a track near Liverpool's Stanley Abattoir.

Another attraction in New Brighton was the outdoor bathing

pool. It seemed huge to us and was full of chemically treated Mersey water. On some of our days out we took flasks of orange squash and sandwiches and sat at the side of the pool watching the annual Miss New Brighton beauty competition. We knew we would never have the figures to compete ourselves, even if we had wanted to, which we most decidedly did not.

As we grew older, my friends and I were allowed to travel on our own even further from the city. Southport, with its fairground and lido, drew us like a magnet in the summer. Again we took our flasks and sandwiches, fondly referred to by us as 'sarnies', for a full day out. We spent endless hours at the Southport Lido going up and down the slide.

After swimming we sometimes played with a blow-up beach ball on the sands. The shops in Lord Street and the Wayfarers Arcade, that years later I found so attractive, were then considered boring by us. Mostly we were satisfied with the beach and the distant views of Blackpool Tower.

We wondered how far the sea went out at Southport. It was often so far away we could not see it from the edge of the beach. However, we did not seek the waves at Southport. Endless lectures from our parents meant we knew the sea was unpredictable. Its behaviour varied from place to place and so it had to be treated with respect. We were never tempted even to paddle at Southport as we felt its sea was too temperamental and odd to be trusted.

Another local example of what I regarded as the sea's oddness was Parkgate on the Wirral. My parents sometimes took Mary and me there. At Parkgate, the Dee estuary seemed to be made entirely of grass, so rare were the high tides. Yet I knew that people in Parkgate went fishing because we were able to buy tiny, delicious shrimps there from the ladies who sat at cottage doors shelling them.

In my memory, it was always sunny at Southport and New Brighton. Strange it is then that both lidos closed, partly because, it was said, bad weather made them uneconomic.

For better or worse?

LITTLE OLD LADIES telling children what to do seemed to be everywhere when I was a child. 'Elbows off the table,' and 'Don't speak with your mouth full,' they ordered at meal times. 'Feet off the seat,' and 'Stand up and let the lady sit down,' they said on trams, buses and trains.

'Don't speak until you are spoken to.' 'Don't interrupt when I am speaking.' 'Children should be seen and not heard.' These were ways to keep children like us quiet.

Woe betide any child who failed so say 'please' or 'thank you' at the right time. Omit just one such word at the end of a sentence, and a little old lady with a disapproving look, aimed not just at you but also at your mother, would remind you firmly of your manners.

Sometimes it seemed that whenever we children were having real fun, a little old lady – a grandmother, a great-aunt and often a total stranger – would pop up to put a damper on things by telling us how naughty we were and how we should behave.

Until he died, my childhood friend Steve Morris never forgot the winter day he and I made the most fantastic slide in the icy snow in front of his house in Cassville Road. It was so glassy and smooth, and we were amazed at our skating skill. We had less than five minutes playing on that slide, until a little old lady with a bag of salt emerged from a nearby house. In an instant, she scattered her salt on our beautiful slide. The ice melted rapidly and we were firmly told off.

The little old ladies seemed to spend a lot of time talking together. They met each other on street corners, on buses, at church and chapel, and in whist drives. Overhearing snippets of their conversation, it seemed to me they agreed on one thing:

that life was much better when they were young. They looked back to a halcyon age when children were better behaved, friendships were stronger, and children learnt more at school.

Well over half a century later, I sometimes feel myself turning into one of those little old ladies. If my grandchildren miss out a 'please' or 'thank you', I am in there like a shot reminding them of their manners. On buses I reprove other children for putting their feet on seats. In the quiet carriages of trains, where there is a ban on the use of mobile phones, I find I am often the first person to complain if somebody uses theirs.

I bemoan the decline in literacy and numeracy that make so many school leavers unemployable. I find myself repeating comments about how primary school teachers might usefully spend less time with glue sticks, stickers, fancy dress and posters, and more time with their times tables and mental arithmetic. I am frequently tempted to comment on the desirability of children concentrating, and concentrating on what a teacher can teach, rather than on 'learning through play'.

I defend rote learning of tables and spellings. I have a tendency to point out that rote learning never did me or my generation any harm – quite the reverse. I wonder why there is a National Curriculum in the schools when, without it, my Liverpool teachers seemed well able to educate my generation, many of whom became the first in their families to go to university.

Quite often I find myself moaning about the NHS. It is all very well to say it is free at the point of need; but it is not – dentists and opticians charge. So many treatments are rationed. It can take ages to get an appointment with some GPs. When they need treatment, NHS patients need it there and then, like private patients. People do not want to be put on long waiting lists. At times I remark that having degrees should not mean nurses think emptying bedpans is beneath them. I become saddened when I see hospital staff chatting about personal matters when they should be working.

And so I think on, but then I pause. I recall that when I was born there was no National Health Service, and that I was five by the time the NHS was created. I recall my mother's weeping terror when I had measles, and her fear that I would be either blind or dead. I think of children clumping along with callipers on their legs to counter the damage done by polio.

I remember that, in my infancy, vaccination and the use of antibiotics were also still in their infancy. I think of my fellow patients in the bronchial ward of Sefton General Hospital coughing, spluttering and dying from the effects of city smog, noxious substances in their working environments, and a lack of knowledge of the harm that can be caused by tobacco.

So when my friends and I begin to moan about how bad things are today, and how much better life was in our youth, I try always to stop and think. True, some things were better then than they are now, but some things were worse then. When I was growing up housework, in particular, was a lot harder.

If she were alive today my grandmother, who was born in the late nineteenth-century, would be amazed at the technology involved in modern housework. The dolly tub, the corrugated metal scrubbing board, and the mangle she used every Monday with great physical effort are gone. Washing machines and electric tumble dryers have replaced them.

The drudgery involved in mid-twentieth-century washdays now features only in pensioners' memories, with dolly tubs, scrubbing boards and mangles now displayed only in museums. Even ironing is less of a chore. Some fabrics do not need ironing and electric irons, particularly steam irons, have made the task a lot easier

Cleaning a home is also less exhausting. Central heating has meant that the daily setting and lighting of fires and cleaning out of grates are for most people distant memories. Black leading the grate with Zebra stove polish, a job my grandmother particularly hated, is long forgotten.

As a teenager I was delighted when the clumsy, wooden Ewbank I unenthusiastically pushed across carpets while doing my share of housework, was replaced by a vacuum cleaner powered by electricity. It was lighter and more effective than the Ewbank. Today, I am even more delighted to own a robot cleaner. I take it into a room, put it on the floor, switch it on, shut the door and leave it to vacuum on its own. How my grandmother would have envied my pieces of technology.

My mother lived long enough to consider television as essential to her life; but, when I was a child, television was very much a mystery. Some people, including my grandmother, thought the sets emitted harmful rays. Consequently, when my parents eventually acquired a TV, it had doors to shut it away when it was not in use.

The choice of TV programmes was very limited then. After we got a television my parents generally confined our family viewing to the current affairs programme *Tonight* with Alan Whicker, Cy Grant, Cliff Michelmore, Derek Hart and Geoffrey Johnson-Smith, and a Welsh programme on Sundays in which Osian Ellis played the harp. Today there are countless choices of programmes, the option of recording programmes and catch-up television. Moreover, a television set is not the only medium on which people can see programmes. Such availability makes it much harder for today's parents to control their children's viewing.

When we moved to Penny Lane, my parents had one item of electrical kitchen technology – a toaster. This was much admired. The toast it produced was always cut in half and the pieces put on the breakfast table in a toastrack. People gave each other toasters as wedding presents then. My parents did not have an electric kettle; instead they boiled water on the gas cooker.

The kitchen gadget my grandmother treasured was the family mincer. It was regularly clamped to the edge of the morning room table. Leftover cooked meat and onions, to form our weekly rissoles or to make mince for shepherd's pie, were pressed through it. The mincer relied for power on my grandmother turning its handle. The only fruits we juiced were lemons and oranges, and the gadget we used to do this was made of glass. Our only other kitchen gadgets – an egg whisk and a can opener screwed to the wall – also depended on human handle-turning for their power.

The lack of electrical machines made cooking slow and boring work. It was also hard for people like my grandmother who suffered from arthritis in her hands. If she were alive today, she would be in awe of the gadgets in my twenty-first-century kitchen: the electric whisk, the microwave, the slow cooker, the food processor, the juicer, and the breadmaker. I can imagine her telling me how much spare time I must have thanks to all the technology.

Our house at Penny Lane had a large larder leading off the kitchen. It was full of cupboards in which pans, dishes, jars and bottles were stored. Above the lower tier of cupboards was a marble slab. It was supposed to help keep fresh food cool. Before fridges and freezers entered people's homes, keeping food fresh was a major problem. Milk, meat, fish, fruit, and vegetables all went off rapidly.

In our larder, flies were kept away from food by covers made of net circles weighted down at the edges by glass beads. Food was bought almost every day, except Sunday when all the shops were shut. My mother enjoyed going to the shops. It was the only aspect of domesticity she did not resent. Her hopes of an academic education had been thwarted, so she was never an enthusiast for housework. She left most of that to my grandmother or to a paid cleaner.

Memory of my mother's hatred of housework is for me a reminder of how greatly things have changed for women. Her father denied her the opportunity of even a secondary education appropriate to her abilities. When I went to the London School of Economics, she regarded that as something she had 'let' me do, and really believed she could have stopped me. In contrast, today, it is widely assumed that girls with the ability will go to university if they want to.

In the mid-twentieth century, the need to make almost daily visits to the shops helped foster a sense of community at a time when that, now overused, word was hardly used in conversation. People got to know each other's business through physical meeting. Very few people had even a landline telephone. Those who did have a phone tended to limit its use to work or emergencies. Urgent messages were often sent by telegrams, delivered by uniformed messengers; they were dreaded as they often contained bad news. Mobile phones, Skype and texting were long into the future.

This meant that, once children went out on their own, it was difficult for their mothers to contact them. The lack of traffic on the roads meant playing in the street was considered safe. Children were encouraged to go outside so that they were not under the feet of their mothers, most of whom were constantly doing housework or making do and mending by knitting or sewing. 'Get from under my feet,' was a regular refrain in many households. Consequently, we were far more independent than most children are today.

Much of the parental time that has been saved by gadgets in the home is now taken up with ferrying children back and forth, usually in cars. Children walking together, parentless, to school have been replaced by the 'School Run', with mother usually driving the car. Activities I enjoyed, like Sunday school and Brownies, have declined. Playing indoors, sitting at a computer, and playing games on a mobile phone or an electronic device have replaced playing out in the street or backyard.

As a young child I was regularly sent out of the back door, told to play out with friends and come back for tea. Since watches were very expensive and no child I knew had a watch until they had taken the 11+, my return was not eagerly anticipated. Parents did not worry about their children's safety like they do today. Children, sent on errands by their mothers or just playing out, were watched over by other local adults who recognised them.

There were few cars, so the streets were full of people walking along, pausing to chat and exchange gossip. In the

Liverpool of my childhood, the sense of community was reinforced by the fact that people tended to remain in the city when they became adults. A son might go away to sea, but he would hopefully return safely home. Few women had careers and most became full-time mothers. Members of families often lived near each other.

In the 1950s, Liverpool parents were usually surprised if their children left the city when they grew up. My mother held it against me that not only had she 'let' me go away to university, but that I had also failed to pay back her generosity because I had not returned to the city after graduating. By the mid-1960s, I was not alone in leaving Liverpool. Thanks to the demands of careers or marriages, my former schoolfriends and many of my cousins were soon scattered around the country. Yet, even today, all of them still feel the pull of the Mersey and their old Liverpool home.

The city of Liverpool has a strong sense of identity. Its children, wherever they live as adults, rarely lose the feeling that it is in Liverpool where they have their roots and really belong. When I suggested to my poor mother, physically frail and suffering from the onset of Alzheimer's, that she should leave the city and come to live near us in west Wales, she was appalled. Pulling herself up to her full shrunken four foot ten, she exploded: 'There is nothing for me there, I AM LIVERPOOL.' I took that as a no.

When my father died a local newspaper headlined his passing with the words 'Death of Mr Liverpool'. The paper was recognising the fact that, as an appointed official of the Liverpool City Council and then as Chief Executive of the short-lived Merseyside County Council, he had devoted his whole adult life to the city. He believed deeply in what he called 'the public service', by which he meant devoting his life to the city of Liverpool and the welfare of its inhabitants.

When I read what has happened to the public service in recent years, I am tempted to moan about the seemingly endless bureaucracy and the current practice of paying senior council officials exorbitant salaries and bonuses just for doing their jobs properly.

I worry too about why there is still child neglect more than sixty years after my friend George, from the Little House, was tied by his mother to a bin in his yard. I cannot understand why there are still terrible housing conditions in parts of Liverpool, yet so many people over the years have done their best to try to improve things.

I find it hard to believe that the ferry across the Mersey is no longer a means of regular transport to Birkenhead and its market, but a tourist boat with its own pop song.

I am pleased that St Monica's home for unmarried mothers, with its judgemental attitudes, has closed. Then, as somebody who raised children as a single parent, I worry that hardly anybody seems to have the courage to tell young people that single parenthood should be avoided if possible, that it is best for children to grow up with two parents living together amicably and that life as a single parent is really hard work.

I worry too about the Family Court's attempts to deal with the problem of what used to be called 'broken homes'. Its increasing tendency to put each parent's right to equal contact with their offspring above child welfare considerations or the protection of previously abused partners risks creating a generation of very insecure human beings. Ordering children to live alternately in their mother's home one week and their father's home the next week is, I believe, most unlikely to make those children feel secure and balanced.

Then I try to tell myself to stop worrying. I reprove myself for thinking like a little old lady. The breakdown of family and community is a worry to people of all ages. I remind myself that some things get better and some worse, and everything changes.

Liverpool has changed. Docks and warehouses, where my grandfathers worked, have become places for people to live and tour around. Many of the shops I knew as a child and thought would be there forever have gone. The up-market delicatessen, Cooper's, where my great-Uncle Jack worked; the department store called Bunney's where each December my parents would buy presents for our Christmas tree; Brian Epstein's shop NEMS; Philip, Son & Nephew, the bookshop where I could swop birthday book tokens for *Observer's Books* – all these shops are but a fast fading memory. They have been replaced by new ones, which attract shoppers from far away. Today the shopping experience in Liverpool One is spoken of with awe by a new generation.

Liverpool's cultural life is just as exciting as it was when I was growing up and later when my father was involved with encouraging the Everyman Theatre and the Bluecoat Society of Arts. In some ways, the city's cultural life has got more interesting. There are new galleries and museums, including the outstanding Museum of Liverpool at the Pier Head, the Tate Liverpool at Albert Dock and the nearby Merseyside Maritime Museum and Museum of Slavery. The City Museum, now reinvented as the World Museum, and the Walker Art Gallery are still there, though they are no longer run by the City Council. The Welsh Choral is a shadow of its former self, but the Royal Liverpool Philharmonic Orchestra is still thriving.

What has not changed is Liverpool's uniqueness. It is a city with physical and social problems, whose inhabitants and supporters are determined to overcome those problems.

Liverpool is a city that looks outward through the mouth of the Mersey to the wider world. It was a multicultural city before multiculturalism was invented, combining tolerance with a deep sense of Christian commitment expressed in a variety of denominations.

Liverpool is a city that continues to foster creativity in the arts, theatre and music and the world benefits from its cultural diversity. It was noticeable, for example, that at the 2012 Olympics opening ceremony, two key performers had been born in the city: Sir Paul McCartney sang 'Hey Jude' at the end, while Sir Simon Rattle conducted the London Symphony Orchestra playing 'Chariots of Fire'. Daniel Craig, who as James

Bond parachuted into the arena with 'the Queen', grew up over the water on the Wirral, but seems to have been affected by the Liverpool spirit.

Liverpool is a city with a sense of humour and that is why it produces so many comedians. Humour is an equaliser; it is Liverpool's greatest asset. I miss sharing it with others when I am away from the city. That sense of humour deflates the self-important and enables people of different backgrounds and experiences to relate to each other.

A sense of humour enables people to cope with a world in which some things get better and some get worse, but everything changes. In exile, I am glad my Scouse sense of humour accompanied me when I moved first to London and then to west Wales. It helps to cope with life's vicissitudes. Thank you Liverpool.

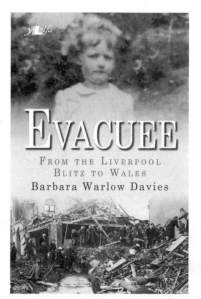
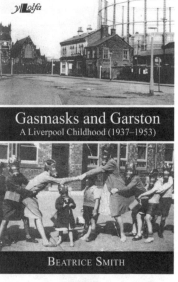